Selling Sno
Achieving Financial Independence
Through Shaved Ice

AARON MAYOVSKY

CONTENTS

Introduction and Acknowledgements

Shortly after I met Ron he told me to just wait for the day that I was "running around collecting twenty five hundred a day" from my *Shaved Ice* shacks. I believed every word he said about the business up to that point, but not because I thought he was lying to me. I doubted his claim because the possibility seemed so unreal to me at the time. After all, twenty five hundred dollars is a lot of money. When the proverbial day actually arrived and the bar of future expectation was raised to levels previously unfathomable, I fully understood that Ron wasn't just some guy blowing smoke one day in the shop. He was teaching me, mentoring me, guiding me to that moment when your entire paradigm just shatters and you realize what a ridiculous fool you were to ever underestimate yourself. For that I am eternally grateful.

Since that day, if I had a nickel for every time I heard someone comment that what I do for a living was "a good idea" I would be a millionaire. So many people (some regular customers, some total strangers) have sincerely approached me with the desire for information about getting started in the *Shaved Ice* business that I couldn't honestly tell you what the number is. Quite simply it's daunting. After selling many more than one turn-key setup to good, hard-working people I can say with some degree of certainty that demand for ownership of a profitable small business in America 2015 is higher than I ever imagined it would be. Now, more than ever, entrepreneurial-minded folks are looking to leave employment behind and go into business for themselves. I believe they represent a market, *the* market, for a solid and profitable small business idea in this country. I believe their numbers are larger than at any time in American history. And if I'm to be perfectly honest, that is why I wrote this book.

It is still possible to make a living owning your own simple small business in America. It is possible to do so with an initial investment of around ten thousand dollars and perhaps much less. It is possible to see a one hundred percent *Return on Investment* after your first month in business. There are no rah-rah seminars to attend, no entrance fee to pay, no pyramids to be found. Best of all, every single one of your new customers will smile in your face and sincerely thank you for what you've just sold them. I know that what I've just written is true because I've done it. It requires no formal education or degree, only a simple willingness to learn how to prepare a product properly, that is to say, to your customer's demands.

Bob Proctor has wisely stated that God's gift to you is more talent and ability than you could ever hope to use. I don't care if you believe in any religion's version of God or no God at all, but his statement about you (yes, *you*) possessing more talent and ability than you could ever hope to use rings so loudly with truth that I believe it's undeniable. I hope it helps you block out every naysayer you will encounter in your life.

Thank you to Tropical Sno for providing an amazing product as well as an amazing team of people to work with. Thank you for allowing me to use your image and logo for this book. I know I'm leaving many people out when I thank Kimberly, Brikelle, Clint, and Don specifically, and for that I apologize.

I am also eternally grateful to each and every person who has ever worked for me. I could not have built my business without you. My only regret (with some of you anyways) is that I couldn't have paid you more. An extra special thank you goes to

Suzanna Healy for helping me with pictures.

Last, but certainly not least, I owe a debt of gratitude to my family, especially my mom, grandma, and brother. Thank you for believing in me. I couldn't have done it without you.

Aaron Mayovsky

With the exception of Ron and Darlene, and to insure their privacy, all names used in this book have been changed.

1

"Fortis Fortuna adiuuat..."

(Fortune favors the bold...)

- Terence, Phormio, 203

What is *Financial Independence?*

Financial Independence is a subjective term; it means different things to different people. Personally, I like to define *Financial Independence* as having enough money to behave independently, or free from coercion, when it comes to issues of money and financial assets. If that's not descriptive enough for you, consider that *Financial Independence* is the ability to wake up in the morning at an hour of your choosing and dedicate your efforts to whatever your mind can conceive. It's the peace of mind that comes with knowing you don't have to work for someone else in order to survive because your assets are working for you, providing you with enough income to live comfortably. It's having the time and money to properly take care of your physical health. It's having enough spare capital to invest in an opportunity when it presents itself. It's the idea of private ownership and private property. Sadly, it is not common sense which is one factor explaining why there are so many financial hacks preying on so many people. That being said, I am not a "financial advisor". This is not a financial advice book. I would never presume to tell you how to best invest your money. That is for you to decide, hopefully after plenty of research and education. This is the story of how I became *Financially Independent* and, more importantly, how I stay that way. My goal in telling it is to get you to think about how you might also become *Independent*, assuming we share that ambition.

Employment and *Financial Independence*

I can't stress the importance of the following sentence enough: **There is absolutely nothing wrong with being employed**. The fact remains that the overwhelming majority of people in America are employed by someone. However, employment and *Financial Independence* tend to work in opposite directions. That is to say the more *Financially Independent* I am the less likely I am to be employed. There are exceptions of course and this begs the question, can someone with a regular job (or career) be *Financially Independent*? The answer is yes, if they work for no other reason than to alleviate boredom. But this is where my definition gets particular. If they're selling their precious time or labor because they genuinely "need the money" they **are not** *Financially Independent*. The *Financially Independent* person is never in need of a job. They tend to work because they desire the experience the job will provide. If your quality of life and current financial situation are entirely dependent upon you being employed then obviously you **are not** *Financially Independent*. If you would be destitute in a month (or a year) as a result of losing your job today you **are not** *Financially Independent*. By definition you are **dependent**.

9

"Maybe it'll stop you trying to be so desperate about making more money than you can ever use? You can't take it with you, Mr. Kirby."

- Grandpa, You Can't Take it With You, 1938

So you might as well blow it all now, right? I always cringe when I hear this rationalization being coughed up, usually by someone who is broke or heavily in debt. As you might suspect I'm an advocate of living frugally, or within your budget. *Financial Independence* doesn't mean filthy rich (though it can), it means the ability to choose. Naturally, the choices we make are very important to the overall goal of achieving *Financial Independence*. Always keep in mind that you can spend whatever you want when you can afford it. Until then it would be wise to exercise some financial discipline. And it can be done much less painfully than you might think. Here are a few suggestions where to begin: avoid frivolous, impulsive purchases like the upgrading of your smartphone or tablet every six months and be amazed as thousands of saved dollars magically appear before your eyes. Invest in a cappuccino or espresso machine for your home and marvel at all the money you didn't spend at Starbucks as it makes a fashionably late appearance to the *Financial Independence* party. Better yet, just drink old-fashioned coffee with cream. Learn to cook and enjoy fresh, whole foods in your kitchen. Stand in awe at the mirror and observe as both you and your wallet become healthier, thanks to that genetically modified, five-layer gut bomb you've been avoiding. The examples one can offer are nearly endless. I'm guessing that with five minutes and a pencil you could come up with even more ways to behave frugally tailored to your specific situation.

Perhaps while you're making your list you could put some

thought into what the word *employment* really means. To me, *employment* means that I'm voluntarily selling a time-slot of my life to someone else. If I want to keep my job I must use my time as *they* see fit. I don't get to take it back. It's gone forever. My quest for *Independence* didn't honestly begin until I became sick of selling my time for so little. Furthermore, it wasn't until I went into business for myself that I fully grasped this concept. More accurately, my quest for *Independence* didn't begin until I came to appreciate that regardless of how many people regurgitate the worn out cliché, time is **not** money. Money is a means of exchange. Time is an irreplaceable asset, and in cases of *employment* it is usually paid for with money. It may seem like semantics at first (after all, to the person earning X dollars per hour time can easily appear to be money) but I assure you the distinction is crucial. Of the two commodities *time* is assuredly the most valuable and the only true measure of one's wealth.

"Wealth is a person's ability to survive so many number of days forward. Or, if I stopped working today, how much longer could I survive?"

- Buckminster Fuller

I'm a big proponent of working "for yourself" as opposed to working for "someone else" but I'm also aware that not everyone is a journeyman or entrepreneur. *Financial Independence* doesn't mean working "for yourself", though it tends to start out that way. It also tends to start out with a hunger for financial knowledge and instructional/motivational material. Consuming that material is crucial. It is one of the first steps you can take in weaning yourself from financial dependency. But it is only the beginning. In the end *Financial Independence* depends less on how much you read and more on how much you *accomplish*, and I'm not about to tell you it's going to be easy. If you aren't set to inherit a profitable business empire, ala Paris Hilton, chances are that you'll have to build one for yourself, perhaps from nothing. This can be very difficult and though not always, it usually means starting with a single small business or investment and committing to long hours of thankless work and research. It can potentially mean years of sacrificing your own desires for the sake of your goal. It definitely means quiet nights at home instead of closing down the local bar every weekend with your bleary-eyed drinking buddies. I'm not against the occasional celebration, but if no one has told you this yet you need to hear it right this minute: a drunk, bloated, hedonistic slob rarely becomes *Financially Independent*. The coveted stratum of *Financial Independence* requires self-control. If you want to be autonomous you must learn to set boundaries. This doesn't mean that the sovereign man or woman can't enjoy a stiff drink once in a while. It simply means that Napoleon Hill had it right when he said that temperance is one of the keys to success…

What *Financial Independence* is not

"A job is a short-term solution to a long-term problem."

- Rich Dad

You might not have been as disgusted as I was when during a town hall meeting in Omaha, Nebraska in 2005 President George W. Bush called a middle-aged woman working three jobs

"Uniquely American". A divorced mother of three children, one of whom was mentally challenged, Mary Mornin had a serious question about the solvency of Social Security. The response coming from the President was typical for a politician, ridiculing and deriding the person asking it while tap-dancing around an actual answer. The exchange went like this:

George W. Bush: "...there's a certain comfort to know that the promises made will be kept by the government. You don't have to worry."

Mary Mornin: "That's good, because I work three jobs and I feel like I contribute."

George W. Bush: "You work three jobs?"

Mary Mornin: "Three jobs, yes."

George W. Bush: "Uniquely American, isn't it? I mean, that is fantastic that you're doing that." (Applause.) "Get any sleep?" (Laughter.)

It was meant as a compliment, and like most drivel of this type it was intended to inspire feelings of pride, patriotism, and (ironically) rugged independence. The audience in attendance cheered enthusiastically while waving their hand-held American flags. It appeared to me that they were applauding the idea of their own bondage. And yet I could not feel sorry for them. Why not? Because while slavery is not *"Uniquely American"*, nor is it something to be proud of, for nearly everyone it is a choice and they have every right to make it.

Wage Slavery

A little clarification: I use the term *wage slavery* differently than most and only then to describe the financial reality that exists for most people. It certainly existed for me. Before I became *Financially Independent* I was a *wage slave*. Burdened by debt and tied to a job I lived paycheck to paycheck, paying my debts and spending what was left on anything I wanted. I knew I should be saving for "retirement" and I was through my 401k. I absolutely loved the company I worked for, and of course I worked for them by choice. However, like most I simply accepted the status quo for exactly what it is: the way things are. At that time the possibility of becoming my own employer, including all the responsibility naturally hitched to that phrase, never occurred to me. Neither did it occur to me to question the solvency of such things as huge financial institutions or government schemes such as Social Security, Medicaid, and Medicare; the three of which I have taken to calling the *Trifecta of Entitlement*. I believed that taking out a mortgage on a house meant I owned it. Whipping out my credit card to pay for the latest iToy I would tell myself that I was "building up my credit". Chugging the Kool-Aid like nearly everyone else I knew, I had complete faith in my lack of financial literacy. I defined "financing" as stretching payments out over time to make them "affordable". It never occurred to me that I was really just borrowing money I didn't have.

When banking giants Lehman Brothers and Bear Stearns collapsed, the precipitating bank failures of the 2008 recession, a rapid series of events forced me to shift my paradigm dramatically. The monolith responsible for my employment was crumbling before my eyes and talking about bankruptcy. My once robust 401k had shed two thirds of its weight, seemingly overnight. The shares of company stock I owned for thirty dollars apiece were trading for less than three. The dealership I loved, once packed with eager families shopping for a new Chevy, was struggling to sell an oil change. People openly cheered the death of the American Auto Industry as a whole and some of them made points I could not ignore. For me, the indebted wage-slave, the revelation that I was financially dependent on a business model which was about to collapse sunk in like a hot knife.

Prudence

"The rich rule over the poor, and the borrower is servant to the lender."

- Proverbs 22:7

In this book I speak openly about my experiences as both employee and employer. I went from seriously indebted wage slave, to struggling self-employed rebel, to *Financially Independent* business owner in the span of 6 years. While I would never claim to know everything there is to know about becoming successful, I've learned a few lessons along the way. One of those lessons was the importance of becoming *Prudent*. You might prefer the term *Frugal*. As long as you commit to becoming one of them your chances of achieving *Independence* will increase greatly. This is difficult to do sometimes because as humans we tend to be influenced by others. It's easy to get caught up in the moment and make imprudent decisions. But our impulses *can* be controlled and it's up to no one but us to do the controlling. Personally, one of the defining moments on my path to *Independence* was mastering the art of recognizing potentially imprudent situations and skillfully avoiding them, or at least taking precautions to protect any lonely dollars that might be hiding in my wallet. An example:

If you've ever been around a bullpen of successful salesman (guys making eight to ten thousand dollars or more per month) you know there's always a little ego present in the room. If they're young and energetic you might have a problem on your hands. After becoming one of these successful salesmen and making a few friends during my tenure as a car salesman I was invited to go out drinking with the pissy, vinegary boys one weekend after work. I think I brought a hundred dollars with me, which turned out to be my protection. Little did I anticipate that "drinking with the boys" entailed limo rides from bar to bar, a growing entourage of thirsty, attractive (and mysteriously broke) young women, debauchery I dare only *mention*, and a general sense of sparing no expense for the whole ordeal. I watched in amazement as some of the flashiest and most successful salesmen I worked with dropped as much as twenty five hundred dollars for a night of thrills without a second thought as to what they were doing. The following Monday I asked a couple of "the boys" how they felt about spending that much money on a single nights' frivolities. Surprisingly no one cared. Even more surprisingly most of them couldn't wait to do it again the following weekend. The moral of the story? Apart from the Johnny Walker judgment, it was lack of discipline that contributed to these young fools and their money parting ways. The pity I felt as I watched them was the subtle teacher holding my hand through the lesson.

Prudence means to discriminate heavily in your affairs, always keeping in mind what's best for you. The prudent, *Financially Independent* person doesn't blow their entire paycheck on a single drunken night of thrills they can barely remember. They possess self-control and exercise it frequently when dealing with their compulsive urges. They usually have plenty of money, they just don't flaunt it. They understand this makes them a mark for would-be looters of the type we will discuss in the second chapter. Often they make large purchases very grudgingly, only when necessary or when to do so could be considered an investment. They likely have no credit cards or almost never use the ones they do have. They pay cash. They don't *"finance"* fifth wheels, jet skis, snowmobiles or dirt bikes. They are content to live in a modest home that's paid for rather than borrow heavily to keep up with the Joneses' and their McMansion. They pay cash for a car they can afford rather than *"finance"* one they can't for the sake of image or comfort or just plain stupidity. In my case, I choose to live in a modest home and drive a ten year old vehicle. I own them both and possess the titles. My home sits in a secluded neighborhood by the river with a blessedly few peaceful neighbors that I rarely see. I couldn't even tell you their names, and I wouldn't want to. *Prudence* includes allowing others the space I demand for myself.

The "Stock Market", "Good Benefits", and the "Minimum Wage"

"I realized from a very early stage that the market is a whole rigged job. There's no chance that investors have in this market."

- Bernie Madoff, infamous Ponzi architect and former chairman of the Nasdaq.

To sum it up once again, *Financial Independence* means that I am not dependent on an employer (or worse, the State) for my financial well-being. It means that I get to spend my time as I choose. It means that I do not have to submit to wage slavery (a job) in order to pay my bills. My small business and modest investments provide a modest income year round so that I may pay my modest expenses. Notice the theme of *Modesty*. It's no accident. If you believe that *Financial Independence* means VIP-status at the local gentlemen's club where you routinely "make it rain" then I submit that you will forever be chasing a pipe dream, and a pathetic one at that.

Financial Independence doesn't mean richer, flashier, more loved and adored, or more famous than everyone else. It means being *fiscally intelligent*. It means using your time and money more wisely than anyone else possibly could. It means allowing the *Walking Dead* you encounter to run their *Rat Race* while complaining about how many people moved their cheese. Allow them to chase their Snookified fantasies of what they believe to be wealth while you focus on the only thing you've ever been able to do anything about: *yourself.* Pay no attention to abstract boogymen like *"Suffering Children"*, *"World Hunger"*, *"Global Warming"*, or any other dubious, exploitative, administration-dominated scheme that's outside of your sphere of influence and designed specifically to play on your guilt and rob you of your money, time, and *Independence*. Instead, be a solid leader, set an example, and become successful yourself. This is the best way to help people better their lives.

"Give a man a fish and you feed him for a day. Teach a man to fish and you feed him for a lifetime."

- Old Chinese Proverb

You've heard of a job with *Good Benefits*, right? For most people *Good Benefits* means that their employer is willing to shell out money for their health insurance and/or contribute to their 401k so they might feel a little better about potentially gambling it all away in the rigged, front-ran, hot-money casino of Dark Pools that everyone laughably calls *"The Stock Market"*. You might have heard that putting your money in *"The Market"* is one of the most tried and true paths to wealth but I have a news flash for you: *"The Stock Market"* is demonstrably rigged by people with **a lot** more money, information, and influence than you. In fact, the thinking person would do well to take notice of the fact that *"The Stock Market"* is where a majority of the especially ghoulish financial predators lurk. I'm not suggesting that you can't make money with a long term plan that includes investing in solid companies with solid balance sheets; you can. I'm not suggesting that I haven't made (and lost) money trading stocks; I have. I'm saying that if you choose to throw money at *"The Stock Market"* you should do your homework, and lots of it, if you don't like watching your dollars perform a disappearing act.

"What's the headline here?"

"The stock market's rigged. The United States stock market, the most iconic market in global capitalism is rigged."

"By whom?"

"By a combination of the stock exchanges, the big Wall Street banks, and high frequency traders."

"Who are the victims?"

"Everyone who has an investment in the stock market."

- Interview between Michael Lewis and Steve Kroft of CBS 60

Minutes discussing Lewis' book, Flash Boys.

In my experience the quickest route to *Financial Independence* is not through the active trading of socks. When properly utilized, stocks are indeed a tool that can boost your net worth. But unless you are a skillful day trader you must be prepared to keep whatever you put in *"The Market"* there for the long haul. *"The Stock Market"* is a dynamic, constantly morphing creature. That's why professional money managers are paid big bucks to monitor it on a daily basis. Though plenty of people trade stocks frequently through their own *Taxable* online brokerage account (think Etrade), the majority of those willing and able to participate in *"The Market"* (a number that currently stands at around 16% of American households) usually purchase stocks with pre-tax dollars and in small tranches of seemingly-safer *Mutual Funds.* If they suddenly need access to this money before they turn 59 ½ years old they can have it, but they are penalized. This is called a *Tax-Privilaged Account*, and there are a few of them to choose from, administered by a dozen different banks and online brokers.

To those of you (like myself) who have participated in *"The Stock Market"* at one time or another I would like to say that because I have no influence in the boardroom of any company listed on the exchanges, and definitely no insider knowledge of events that might initiate a "pop or drop" in any given stock, I consider individual *"Stock Picking"* in *"The Stock Market"* akin to selecting which lottery ticket to scratch. One might be a winner, one might be a loser. The major difference between *"The Stock Market"* and a lottery ticket being that with stocks one domino falling has the potential to tank the entire market or even the world economy. Have you ever heard the term, House of Cards?

"Well the Financials, as I keep saying, are just super bargains. I particularly like Merrill Lynch, which is an astonishingly well run company. [Did] You know a couple of days ago that it was barely trading at seven times earnings? Financials typically trade at a low fee, but this is a joke! They might as well be putting it in cereal boxes and giving it away, that's how cheap it is."

- Ben Stein, pumping Merrill Lynch stock (at $76.04 per share) on the Neil Cavuto Show, August 18th, 2007. Merrill would go on to collapse to $17.05 per share, finally being purchased for $29 per share by Bank of America on September 14th, 2008 in a hasty, Government-arranged bailout.

The second half of the *Good Benefits* equation, the employer-provided health insurance half, should be addressed in light of the fact that it will soon be out of reach for most people. In an instructive display of exactly how much regulation your influence can buy you in contemporary America (and because businesses generally want to minimize their expenses as much as possible) the heavy hitters of American enterprise have broadly supported government schemes forcing you to buy health insurance in a rigged market that they control, schemes like Obamacare. The stuffed suits sitting around the boardroom table understand that their support gives them leverage as to how the law will be implemented because when things don't go their way they can always threaten to pull it. Meanwhile, 30-hour per week thresholds have ensured that examples of employers converting full-time employees to part-time status, for no other reason than to avoid paying the higher health care costs they supported when they were championing Obamacare's implementation, are so numerous and overwhelming that it would take several additional pages to list them here. Their numbers alone are a glaring example of the supposed "Unintended Consequences" of all government welfare.

Now let's turn our attention to a sorely misunderstood topic, the so-called *"Minimum Wage"*. Barry Ritholtz recently provided a textbook example of the prevailing contemporary economic ignorance involving the *"Minimum Wage"*. Dissecting it will provide further insight into why becoming *Financially Independent* is more important now than ever.

Ritholtz published an editorial on the opinion page of Bloomberg Media demonizing companies like Wal-Mart and McDonalds, labeling them *"Welfare Queens"* for setting aside instructional material, resources and time for their employees to take advantage of federal welfare programs. Instead of properly labeling and criticizing the situation as an indictment of massive "entitlement" schemes like Obamacare, SNAP (food stamps), or the *Trifecta of Entitlement* as the direct cause of his ire, Ritholtz attacked both Wal-Mart and McDonalds for (get your hip-waders out) "consuming taxpayer supported aid":

"Wal-Mart, the nation's largest private sector employer, is also the biggest consumer of taxpayer supported aid. According to Florida Congressman Alan Grayson, in many states, Wal-Mart employees are the largest group of Medicaid recipients. They are also the single biggest group of food stamp recipients. Wal-Mart's "associates" are paid so little, according to Grayson, that they receive $1000 on average in public assistance. These amount to massive taxpayer subsidies for private companies."

- Barry Ritholtz, Bloomberg Opinion Page 11/13/13

Flaunting his ignorance of both economics and logic ("public assistance" amounts to massive taxpayer subsidies for *The Poor*, regardless of whether or not they have a job) Ritholtz insists the employer, in this case Wal-Mart, has been consuming their workers' welfare check. Ritholtz doesn't dare calling the actual recipient of the eye-popping figure of one thousand dollars in welfare (the employee) a *"Welfare Queen"*, at least not to their face. That derisive is reserved exclusively for evil employers like Wal-Mart. Not bothering to comprehensively identify a cause to the problem in his piece, Ritholtz is ready with a predictable, knee-jerk solution:

"The simplest solution is to raise the minimum wage. If full-time employees are living below the poverty level--especially those with children—it's no surprise they are going to need public assistance. Raising the minimum wage over a period of time will eliminate much of this corporate welfare. The costs will be slightly higher prices at fast food restaurants and low end retailers.

- Barry Ritholtz, Bloomberg Opinion Page 11/13/13"

Barry is ridiculously wrong about gold, Corporate Taxation, and as I'll be demonstrating, the *"Minimum Wage"* and Corporate Welfare. Even more laughable than his claim that raising the *"Minimum Wage"* will eliminate Corporate Welfare is his lackluster prediction for prices after the fact. Living in his well insulated East Hampton bubble, Barry (who is a well connected money manager and revered columnist/pundit for many entrenched Establishment financial publications) must be suffering from *Affluenza*. He probably isn't bothered by the menial daily chores working middle-class American families face daily such as shopping for their food at "low-end retailers" like Wal-Mart. If he were, he might have noticed that the price of beef and bacon hit an all time high this year while prices on all kinds of food are inflating like crazy even while portion sizes are shrinking. Meanwhile Barry is busy penning articles which preposterously claim that there is no inflation lately, citing hedonically adjusted numbers provided by the Bureau of Labor Statistics that anyone with half a brain knows to be rigged from the starting gate. Keep in mind that the "Corporate Welfare" Barry is decrying is actually individual welfare consumed by people such as Medicaid and food stamps, and he admits as much in his piece. Barry either has no clue what Corporate Welfare actually is, or is willfully misusing this term.

The problem with this parade of fallacies isn't the person presenting them. The problem is that his faulty logic posing as critical thinking is actually believed by *anyone* due to their misunderstanding of basic economics. This is one of the many reasons that a raise in the *"Minimum Wage"* will become a legislated reality in this country in short order, as it is the most politically expedient way to calm the Barrys you see on TV every day. It should come as no surprise that we have seen the president make raising the federal *"Minimum Wage"* a focal point of his remaining time in office. The negative economic effects of a Government Mandated Minimum Wage are an advanced course of study for another day, though suffice it to say that a raise in the *"Minimum Wage"* to any amount will not make you *Financially Independent*. Why not? Because business is more than happy to do what it always does when faced with higher costs: pass that expense on to you, the unwitting consumer. Don't take my word for it though. Just ask once esteemed Economics professor (and now notorious pariah) John Gruber:

"We just tax the insurance companies, they pass it on in higher prices, that offsets the tax break we get, it ends up being the same thing. It's a very clever, you know, basic exploitation of the lack of

economic understanding of the American voter. "

- Jonathan Gruber, MIT economist and so-called "Architect of Obamacare", gloating about how he and like-minded political operatives colluded with politicians to conceal Obamacare's true costs (and effects) from the "American voter" in order to pass the law.

Gruber, the "Architect" of not only Obamacare but Romneycare, might be a despicable Political Mandarin, but he is exactly right about your political leaders manipulating the vast majority's ignorance of basic economics to pass laws that will hurt them and their bank account, which means you and your bank account. All prices will raise around you in tandem. A raise in the *"Minimum Wage"* will only make you a higher paid wage slave, one with the ability to purchase just about the same amount of stuff at higher prices. The constant misinformed chatter one hears surrounding the issue is just another reason to prepare for any eventuality by becoming truly *Financially Independent*, and to do it by any means at your disposal while always keeping in mind that the problem isn't Grubbie per-se but that he and his ilk, like Barry, have any influence over your life at all.

"An error does not become truth by reason of multiplied propagation, nor does truth become error because nobody sees it. "

- Mahatma Gandhi

Plan for the future: Go Bankrupt

A significant element of *Financial Independence* involves planning for the future. By this I mean anticipating real world events and preparing for them, not buying this or that *Mutual Fund* or throwing your money at this or that *"advisor"*. I would never recommend that you listen to any of the cheaply purchased circus freaks passing for *"financial advisors"* in our brave new Federal Reserve dependent world unless they're talking about one thing: debt, and the need to rid yourself of it entirely. If you don't have the slightest clue where to begin your financial planning I would suggest you start there. And remember, while it's true that there exists *"good debt"* and *"bad debt"* the difference between the two is an advanced class for the advanced and *"sophisticated"* investor with money to burn. For the person seeking *Financial Independence* I would like to suggest that **no debt** is the answer. After all, *Financial Independence* and debt are antonyms. One can't be independent financially if they are in bondage through debt. That's a perversion of logic.

If one was burdened debt and looking to become *Independent* the first question I might ask them would be, "What steps do you plan to take today that will help you accomplish your goal of becoming debt free tomorrow?" I would encourage them to be creative and completely ignore the social stigma that is sometimes attached to certain options. One of these options might be the only solution available. I'm speaking specifically here about bankruptcy. Believe it or not, so many "successful" people (including famous businessmen and Hollywood actors) have gone bankrupt that even the mildest inquiry into the subject would blow your mind.

Have you ever heard the name Walt Disney? Did you

know that before he created Mickey Mouse, Walt Disney went bankrupt? Plagued by one bad financial decision after another his first venture, Laugh-O-Gram Studios, was eventually unable to pay employees for the work they had performed. Things got so bad for Walt that he resorted to living in his office, eating beans from a can, and taking baths once a week at the train depot; all in an attempt to save the business which failed in spite of his efforts. Bankrupt and traveling with everything he owned in his pockets and a suitcase, Walt boarded a train for California and his eventual success. Even lesser known however are the myriad financial struggles he experienced throughout his career after he achieved success with the Walt Disney Company. Many people if told so today probably wouldn't believe that Snow White was a hair's breadth away from not seeing completion due to financial complications. When I consider the difference between success and failure I often think about Walt and his tenacity. My belief is that if you are anywhere near as determined as Walt Disney it is only a matter of time before you achieve *Financial Independence.*

2

"Do you ask what moral obligation I owe to my fellow men? None – except the obligation I own to myself, to material objects, and to all of existence: rationality."

- John Galt

Your Civic Duty

You might be confused if you've never heard the term *Civic Duty* before. Beware anyone who uses it seriously. When used seriously it's employed by those looking to separate you from your money using any form of dubious logic they think will appeal to your emotions. The idea that you were born with *original debt* might be a canard, but it is more widely believed than the idea that you were born with *original sin*. In fact, it's the one thing people of all creeds can agree on. Any disagreement revolves around how much you supposedly owe. Another point of total agreement is that you owe taxes (fealty) to the State (by *State* I mean the *Government*) for no other reason than you live within its borders. If you're financially productive within those borders or even worse, an employer, watch out. You're an especially easy target, ultra-susceptible to demonization by the self-righteous hoards who've never built a thing in their life. You might have thought you were listening to Lenin rallying the Bolsheviks (or more recently Venezuelan president Felipe Maduro as he sends in the Army to nationalize another industry) but it was actually recently elected Senator and unabashed Collectivist Elizabeth Warren who shrieked in 2012,

"There is nobody in this county who got rich on their own. Nobody. You built a factory out there, good for you. But I want to be clear: you moved your goods to market on roads the rest of us paid for. You hired workers the rest of us paid to educate. You were safe in your factory because of police forces and fire forces that the rest of us paid for. You didn't have to worry that marauding bands would come and seize everything at your factory. Now look, you built a factory and turned it into something terrific, or a great idea. God bless. Keep a hunk of it. But part of the underlying social contract is you take a hunk of that and pay forward for the next kid who comes along."

- Elizabeth Warren, August, 2012

That "underlying social contract" she's talking about is your *Civic Duty*. Never mind that the "workers the rest of us paid to educate" were also paid a wage they agreed to in exchange for whatever labor they performed. You could have (and should have) paid them more you rich business owner, you can afford it. Assuming you've never contributed a cent in taxes or toward welfare, she insists that everyone else in the world has paid for all the modern luxuries of civilization you take for granted and therefore they have a righteous lien on all of your productive efforts for the rest of your life. The ridiculousness of a member of an exclusive, well-protected club (the Senate) claiming to have personally opened up her wallet to shell out money for every road you've ever driven on is not addressed. Neither is the fact that "the next kid who comes along" is actually the State's myriad confiscation bureaus and they've actually been here the whole time. Speaking of assumptions, I can only imagine that when it comes to her taxes the benevolent Ms. Warren (who in terms of personal income resides in the oft-maligned 1%) has a team of accountants handling them, making sure she pays every cent and writes off nothing. She's a humble, altruistic public servant after all. Just don't call her wealthy.

Rejecting the charade

"Run for your life from any man who tells you that money is evil. That sentence is the leper's bell of an approaching looter."

- Francisco D'Anconia

The most recent example of what to expect when *Civics*-minded people come to power is the breathtaking transformation of the city of Detroit during the last sixty and especially the last twenty years. Once an industrial powerhouse and the fifth largest city in America, present day Detroit is a depressing shadow of its former self. Finally allowed to declare bankruptcy after a long legal battle with pensioners and unions collectivized against the taxpayers they supposedly served all those long years in city government, Detriot 2014 can only be described as a severely bankrupt freak show:

- *Since 2000, Detroit's population has declined 26 percent.* There are now just 706,000 people in the city, way down from 1.85 million during its industrial heyday in 1950.

- *The official unemployment is now 18.6 percent* and fewer than half of the city's residents over the age of 16 are working. Per capita income is an extremely low $15,261 a year, which means there's not all that much tax revenue pouring in.

- *Low tax revenue, in turn, means that city services are suffering.* Detroit has the highest crime rate of any major city, and fewer than 10 percent of crimes get solved. The average response time for an emergency call is 58 minutes. Some 78,000 buildings are abandoned or blighted and there are an estimated 12,000 fires every year. About 40 percent of the city's street lights don't work.

- *High crime and blight are driving even more residents out of the city.* It's also driving down property values, which means many residents have stopped paying property taxes. The city collected about 68 percent of the property taxes owed in 2011. Both of those things put a further strain on Detroit's finances.

- *Detroit is sagging under decades of bad governance.* "The city's operations have become dysfunctional and wasteful after years of budgetary restrictions, mismanagement, crippling operational practices and, in some cases, indifference or corruption,"

- *Meanwhile Detroit owes around 18.5 billion to its creditors.* That includes about $6 billion in health-care and life insurance obligations, plus roughly $3.5 billion in pension costs racked up over the years. Given its ever-worsening economic slide, Detroit was in no position to pay off all its obligations.

"Detroit just filed for bankruptcy. Here's how it got there."

- *Washington Post Wonkblog, Brad Plummer, July 18, 2013*

It can be argued that Detroit is a microcosm of the economic situation in America as a whole, only nationwide the problem is much worse. The National Debt and size of government have actually gone exponential. Some economists contend (and I agree with them) that the National Debt will never be repaid and will eventually have to be repudiated.

Understanding such things leads to certain questions. Perhaps you've even considered them yourself but haven't had the gumption to ask them out loud or share them with your colleagues. I can't say I blame you for that. The belief that everyone needs to "Pay Their Fair Share" is as widely held as it is deeply held. There is no need to subject yourself to unwanted scrutiny by declaring that you're in opposition to the status-quo while standing around the water cooler one day. I would not advise you to take up a YouTube channel and start screaming about your political beliefs. There's definitely no need to speak to anyone about your taxes (with the exception of a qualified individual who is helping you to minimize them). All of that only leads to eventual confrontation with the State and its aforementioned collection agencies. Besides, your chances of changing someone's mind are practically zero. My advice is that you don't waste the time or effort. The answer lies within yourself, and it is nothing less than the complete rejection of the idea that you are somehow responsible for paying for this charade.

"It is not from the benevolence of the butcher, the brewer, or the baker that we expect our dinner, but from their regard to their own interest."

- Adam Smith, The Wealth of Nations, 1776

This is tough to do sometimes. The clueless collectivists who couldn't care less about how their free goody is paid for are out there, and in America 2015 their numbers are stunning. Sometimes it seems as if they outnumber thinking people two hundred million to one. The clued-in collectivists include the present Administration and its appointees whose agenda is nothing less than the creation of a European style cradle-to-grave welfare State, and they are impressively close to it. Their "Public Relations" machine includes nearly every media outlet and all of their spokesmen. Actual journalists who dare to step outside the orchestrated political narrative are demonized. The political elite know that they can rely on the support of many teachers whose religious faith in collectivism affects their world view, subject matter, and behavior even down to the elementary school level. Support for the idea of collectivism is heavy among most unionized workers and so many people receiving welfare benefits, which means the hard-working, consistently voting soccer mom right down the street from you. She deserves welfare, if for no other reason than "times are tough" and she's raising a couple of babies sans Daddy. Kids are the future, haven't you heard? Besides, you have the money to spare. Soccer mom doesn't care about cities or countries going bankrupt. She's never heard of a logical fallacy and as long as the food stamps keep coming she never will. Because in the end nothing is more important than "The Children" having enough fill-in-the-blank, isn't it? If it means you pay a little more in taxes here and there, well, that's just the way it has to be.

This is your *Civic Duty*, the price you pay for living in The Greatest County in the World. Just ask the president. Backing up Ms. Warren's comments in a stump speech in Roanoke, Virginia during his re-election campaign President Barack Obama said,

"There are a lot of wealthy, successful Americans who agree with me – because they want to give something back. They know they didn't – look, if you've been successful, you didn't get there on your own. You didn't get there on your own. I'm always struck by people who think, well, it must be because I was just so smart. There are a lot of smart people out there. It must be because I worked harder than everybody else. Let me tell you something – there are a whole bunch of hardworking people out there."

"If you were successful, somebody along the line gave you some help. There was a great teacher somewhere in your life. Somebody helped to create this unbelievable American system that we have that allowed you to thrive. Somebody invested in roads and bridges. If you've got a business – you didn't build that. Somebody else made that happen. The Internet didn't get invented on its own. Government research created the Internet so that all the companies could make money off the Internet."

- President Barack H. Obama, July 13, 2012

That's right. "Somebody else made that happen." And the Government created the Internet out of pure altruism so that you might make money. We won't go into that laughable Internet claim (or the Internet's true military origins) so long as you understand that unspecified "Somebody Else" is personally responsible for your well being. To question their benevolent claim on your energy and efforts is not within the acceptable realm of discussion. Therefore you owe them money. Even in the zombified horror-show of America 2012 this ideology did not go un-protested. Sadly, the champions of Individualism, Liberty, and sound economics were largely ignored by what passes for the Media in this country and the president sailed smoothly to a re-election on a platform of increasing taxes on the exact same business owners he spoke so eloquently about.

"Any power must be an enemy of mankind which enslaves the individual by power and force, whether it arises under the Fascist or the Communist flag. All that is valuable in human society depends upon the opportunity for development accorded to the individual."

- Albert Einstein

The real 99%

One of the many sad realities of *Civics* is that the legions of uninformed and apathetic among us vastly outnumber those who are aware of economics, logic, and reality. Sometimes it seems as if you could correctly place their numbers at 99%. Though an argument could be made against their intelligence the truth is that "The 99%" of uninformed people have been duped into believing the outright lies being peddled by the politicians they eagerly elected. Their politicians' images are bolstered by the media's portrayal of them as anything but what they really are, which is a club of lying thieves who are literally grabbing at every last dollar you will ever earn with both hands, while at the same time regarding you contemptuously as too stupid to know what's in your best interest. Though please, once again, don't take my word for it,

"This bill was written in a tortured way to make sure CBO did not score the mandate as taxes. If CBO [Congressional Budget Office]

scored the mandate as taxes, the bill dies. Okay, so it's written to do that. In terms of risk rated subsidies, if you had a law which said that healthy people are going to pay in – you made explicit healthy people pay in and sick people get money, it would not have passed...Lack of transparency is a huge political advantage. And basically, call it the stupidity of the American voter or whatever, but basically that was really really critical for the thing to pass...Look, I wish Mark was right that we could make it all transparent, but I'd rather have this law than not."

- John Gruber, "Architect of Obamacare/Romneycare", explaining how a law enabling the Government to force you to purchase health insurance ("the mandate") could not be sold to Congress as a tax or else the bill would die. Scandalously, John Roberts, Chief Justice of the Supreme Court, would go on to singlehandedly decide that "the mandate" was a tax, and was therefore Constitutional.

When the president says that rich people "agree with him" and want to "give something back" the majority of people unquestioningly lap it up, thanks in large part to the Federally Licensed Mainstream Media's portrayal of the message. It occurs to a scant few of them that something might be going on behind the scenes when they're witnessing a bribe being passed off as a "donation" which is what it's all about of course, deception. Buying a little more time to keep the game going a little bit longer.

Passing off a bribe

"It's a f---ing valuable thing, you just don't give it away for

nothing."

- Disgraced former Illinois governor Rod Blagojevich referring to the vacant senate seat once occupied by Barack Obama.

In March, 2011, the New York Times published an instructive article meant to demonize the Politically-Connected General Electric, and its even more well-connected CEO Jeffery Immelt, for doing what every American business with even an ounce of self-preservation does: structuring the company's taxes in such a way as to minimize them, in some cases holding vast sums of money in overseas bank accounts to avoid U.S. taxes. The surprise was not that the Times would be offended by such behavior. Rather, it was that they would publish the article at all because in a fleeting moment of authentic journalism the author stumbled upon the actual method (and the actual scandal) by which most decisions are arrived at in Washington D.C., pay for play bribery.

To sum up the situation, GE had a lucrative tax shelter that was being threatened by pending legislation. For many smaller companies this could have spelled trouble. However, GE is a little more Politically-Connected than the average bear. So much that,

The head of its tax team, Mr. Samuels, met with Representative Charles B. Rangel, then chairman of the Ways and Means Committee, which would decide the fate of the tax break. As he sat with the committee's staff members outside Mr. Rangel's office, Mr. Samuels dropped to his knee and pretended to beg for the provision to be extended – a flourish made in jest, he said through a spokeswoman.

That day, Mr. Rangel reversed his opposition to the tax break, according to other Democrats on the committee.

The following month, Mr. Rangel and Mr. Immelt stood together at St. Nicholas Park in Harlem as G.E. announced that its foundation had awarded $30 million to New York City schools, including $11 million to benefit various schools in Mr. Rangel's district. Joel I. Klein, then the schools chancellor, and Mayor Michael R. Bloomberg, who presided, said it was the largest gift ever to the city's schools.

- The New York Times, March 24th, 2011

I can't say for certain that this "award" had anything to do with the benevolent Rep's vote on that particular bill. That would just be cynical. The man probably just had a change of heart. And clearly the creeps involved weren't in on the whole charade. They never are. Only cynical people think that way, cynical people who want to shirk their *Civic Duty*. These are the same people who understand that this is the way things have been and will be for a long time. The question these cynical people might ask themselves while they ponder the hopelessness of the situation is simply, "What can I really do about it?"

"Consider just one example: Dennis Hastert was a jovial ex-high school wrestling coach and member of the Illinois House of Representatives when he was first elected to Congress in 1986. Through hard work, attention to detail, and a knack for coalition building, he rose to be Speaker of the House in 1999 and served until 2007, when he resigned. When Hastert first went to congress he was a man of relatively modest means. He had a 104 acre farm in Shipman, Illinois, worth between $50,000 and $100,000. His

other assets amounted to no more than $170,000. He remained at a similar level until he became Speaker of the House.

But by the time he set down the Speaker's gavel, he was substantially better off than when he entered office, with a reported net worth of up to $11 million. "

- Throw Them All Out: How Politicians and Their Friends get Rich Off Insider Stock Tips, Land Deals, and Cronyism That Would Send The Rest Of Us To Prison, Peter Schweitzer, 2010

A tax by any other name: Income vs. Capital Gains

"He has erected a multitude of New Offices, and sent hither swarms of Officers to harass our people, and eat out their substance. "

- The Declaration of Independence

One of the main incentives to start a business is that individuals and businesses are taxed in different ways and in different amounts. If you've ever "financed" anything you've probably been asked what you earn "before taxes" as opposed to what you make "after taxes" (your *Gross* vs. *Net* income). Businesses are not exactly taxed like that. Generally speaking businesses are taxed at a lower rate than people and they only pay tax on the money they earn *after expenses*. The obligations of the business owner include reaching into their pocket to match employee contributions to retirement accounts, welfare bureaucracies, tax collection agencies, monopolized insurance cartels and any other Government Scheme eagerly seeking its unearned, undeserved piece of the pie. After the Government has been paid, the remaining income earned by people through their job is taxed via the Income Tax while the income earned by business is taxed via the Capital Gains Tax. Income earned through investments also falls under the Capital Gains Tax. This is not a tax advice book however, so I will only say that you should seek solid advice from a paid professional whose sole concern is the minimization of your tax bill and follow it diligently when dealing with your business and its finances. Tax laws are different by state and change yearly as new opportunities for the beast to feed are identified and exploited. During these changes a good accountant can be worth their weight in gold.

When I'm asked about taxes by someone discussing the purchase of one of my locations, and invariably I am, I always offer some form of the following sage advice,

"...the fact is that if the mafia would come to you and say, 'We want $2000 a month or we're going to hurt you...' I would not advise you not to pay them. Because you may get hurt by not paying them. Whether it's legal or not doesn't necessarily matter. You're gonna get hurt if you don't."

"It's the same thing with the IRS. They can hurt you. They can put you in jail. They can torture you. So if you don't pay them, you may get hurt. So I never advise people not to pay. I tell people, 'Yeah, pay your taxes.'"

- Aaron Russo, 2007

Yes, pay your taxes. But how much longer are you going to contribute to morally questionable and fiscally insolvent Ponzi

Schemes like the *Trifecta of Entitlement* with your precious time and labor? To be sure, you will never fully un-ensnare yourself from the web of fraud and deception. You can be as sure of taxes as you are of death. But you can greatly minimize your exposure through business ownership and wise investments. Hillary Clinton might be an odious elitist, but she was factually correct when she said the "truly well off" don't pay the Income Tax. They don't receive "income" and therefore they are able to avoid the *Trifecta*. Their money comes from profits earned through business or investments that are taxed only once and only when they make a profit. This is the difference between the Income Tax and the Capital Gains Tax and it is no less stark than the difference between knowledge and ignorance. So now that you're knowledgeable, what are you going to do about it?

3

*"...all experience hath shewn, that mankind are more disposed to
suffer, while evils are sufferable, than to right themselves by
abolishing the forms to which they are accustomed. But when a
long train of abuses and usurpations, pursuing invariably the same
Object evinces a design to reduce them under absolute Despotism,
it is their right, it is their duty, to throw off such Government, and
to provide new Guards for their future security."*

– The Declaration of Independence

Taking the Plunge

In many ways the quest for *Financial Independence* is
about soul searching, or figuring out who you want to become.
Some people are perfectly content to work their *Good Job* for as
long as humanly possible, milking every *Good Benefit* for all it's
worth. As long as they're bringing home a decent paycheck and
can provide their family with shelter, food, "health insurance", and
the occasional trinket, they likely *believe* they're independent. It
might not have occurred to them that they're actually *reliant*.
Perhaps it's also never occurred to them that as an employee
they're infinitely replaceable, especially "in times like these" or
when "the economy is bad", their unique skill set be damned.

Maybe they've never bothered to look at their paycheck and realize that they're actually being paid *last,* the government of course being paid *first* thanks to withholdings like the *Trifecta-of-Entitlement* and the second plank of Marx's detestable Communist Manifesto, the Graduated Income Tax. Of course there's the possibility that they've noticed all of these things and still depend on their job as their sole source of income. Most of us have to work to get by. Most of us have no choice but to save what little money we can squirrel away from our job and begin our quest for *Independence* that way. That's certainly how I began. I saved every dollar I could for two years, spending only when I absolutely had to. I planned diligently while I saved and mentally prepared myself for the massive change I knew was coming. I waited for the opportune moment to quit my job and when the time came I did exactly that. With one very brief exception I have not been employed since.

So how did I do it? What steps did I take specifically? How did I summon the intestinal fortitude and mental courage to quit my job and strike out on my own with only a few thousand dollars and a dream? Why did I succeed when so many others with more startup capital and the same type of desire fail miserably? Did I receive some special break from a politically well-connected friend? Was I privy to some secret that few of us know and even fewer are willing to share? Of course not…

"If we could change ourselves, the tendencies in the world would also change. As a man changes his own nature, so does the attitude of the world change towards him. … We need not wait to see what others do."

– Mahatma Ghandi

(Commonly misquoted as, "Be the change you wish to see in the world.")

There are many ideas, and definitely a few books, that have influenced my thinking and behavior during my lifetime. I think now would be an appropriate time to single out two of them and offer a brief explanation of a smattering of the ideas presented therein and how they apply to *Financial Independence.*

The Wealth of Nations rocked the known world when it was published in 1776 if only because it turned so many of the commonly accepted, ridiculous economic theories of the day on their head. It was also highly influential. It is well documented that many of "The Founders" of this country were influenced by the economic philosophy presented by its author Adam Smith. In his book, Smith coined a term and economic idea known as the *Division of Labor* to explain why job tasks become so specialized in the *Labor Market.* No doubt he would be entertained to see his ideas on full display with help from the modern technology of our time. In almost all companies (and definitely in all factories today) we see his philosophy playing out as worker bees, General Managers, and even company owners all perform separate and necessary tasks demanding separate and necessary skills. Their collective effort enables their company to succeed by producing a product or service and offering it for sale at a profit.

In *The Cashflow Quadrant,* Robert Kiyosaki goes into painstaking detail outlining what I like to call the *Division of Mindset* in a brilliant, easy to understand manner that has worked wonders in helping me decipher people and their true motivations. The *Division of Mindset* simply means that some people will always be content to be an employee while some people never will. Among the ranks of the former are a few who aspire to be managers or regional directors but most are happy simply being effective worker bees. These folks value things such as *"Job Security"* but want nothing to do with the responsibilities of owning the business and the success or failure that comes with it. Among the latter are well known investors, CEOs, and entrepreneurs. Their rugged individualism and refusal to compromise their vision stands in stark contrast to their docile employees. As you might imagine the number of willing employees is *far greater* than those who would take a calculated risk in the hopes of becoming *Financially Independent* through means such as business ownership or the risk of investing. It seems that this arrangement would work out nicely, and indeed it does, though not always to everyone's liking.

Humility

"People don't get rich by doing certain things. They get rich by doing things in a certain way."

– Bob Proctor

I might not be a Hindu, but I firmly believe in the idea of *Karma.* I believe that if you enter into a business relationship with positive karma, always producing something of value in return for the money you expect, you will achieve the best results possible. This can especially be said of employment. Have you ever noticed who tends to get the promotion? If you answered the most productive person on the team you would (in most cases anyway) be right. Likewise, if you enter into an arrangement looking to take advantage of someone, and are successful in doing so, don't be surprised when someone takes advantage of you down the road. Karma dictates that you had it coming.

A word about humility is in order here. Unlike Russell Brand, I am an Individualist. I hold to the belief that every person is not only capable of, but responsible for shaping their own destiny. If employment sounds good to you or will meet your current goals, pursue it. I know I'm immensely thankful for every single employee that I've ever had. I know I wouldn't have been able to pursue my own goal of *Financial Independence* without first having a job, and a good one, which enabled me to save enough money to feel confident as I leapt from my nest of comfort. This book is not meant to convert you to my every way of thinking. It's not up to the sovereign man to convert anyone to his way of thinking. That's pure belligerence. Instead, I've chosen to lead by example and plant in the minds of those I meet the *idea* of *Independence* through prudent and persistent action. When people ask me about my business or how much money I make I politely inform them that I've not been employed for a number of years and I make enough to get by. I don't bloviate about owning a business like some self-righteous ass with deeper than believable pockets. This is a much more effective way not only to spread the idea of *Financial Independence*, but to live out the creed of *Independence* as well. Finally, keep in mind that many people will choose employment over business ownership, especially when they're faced with the prospect of building something out of nothing or very little. The world is very scary after all and what I perceive to be the chains of employment can be thought of by some (most actually) as the security of a seat belt. A person's perception depends on where they are on their own journey to *Independence,* if they decide to ever take that journey at all. So be humble when you deal with all people regarding all things. I have no doubt that if you're reading these words a streak of *Independence* and self-reliance is already coursing through your veins. Just don't mistake that for superiority. It's nothing more that the essence of life, and it's felt by both freemen and wage-slave, though to differing degrees I'll admit.

I took *The Plunge* after many years of employment. I began working in my grandparent's restaurant when I was thirteen years old. I started out at $4.25 an hour, which was the *"Minimum Wage"* at that time. For two years prior to that I rose well before the crack of dawn to work my own neighborhood, and the surrounding neighborhoods as a paperboy, a considerable route. My wage was a fat, hearty zero dollars. In fact, my pay was dependant on how many monthly subscription payments I was able to collect from my neighbors. I still remember taking home more than one plate of cookies or fudge that had been left out on a step or porch for me around Christmas time. I considered that as part of my pay, and it was. I worked almost full-time consistently through high school and up until graduation. I washed dishes in a high-end restaurant inside an exclusive resort and fielded complaints in a call center while attending college classes full-time. My obsession/addiction to money even caused me to take the pursuit of it to further, more dubious lengths.

For as long as I can remember I have been mesmerized by money and consumed by the pursuit of it. When I was a teenager and first coming to grips with the experiment in socialization that we all lovingly call high school, one of the things I immediately noticed was that the popular kids smoked pot. It wasn't long before I figured out that they spent a majority of their money on it as well. Soon I was doing what any entrepreneur would do, networking with clients and supplying them with what they demand. I became so successful that I attracted the attention of the local police, and as a result I was constantly in trouble with the law. My success continued through college (a movie was recently filmed personifying my high profile dealer). Shortly after I earned my Associates Degree, and just before my 21st birthday, I was on my way to prison for selling marijuana. After serving two years of a five year sentence and completing a dubious, intensive, humiliating, laughably mis-named nine month in-patient drug treatment program called a *"Therapeutic Community"* I was released. One of my first priorities (and a requirement of my parole) was to find a job. I found a very good one as a car salesman and worked it diligently for three years before giving it up to pursue my dream of owning my own business, my own gold mine. But before I get ahead of myself allow me to take you on a tour of Crazytown...

Crazytown: Capital of Prisonyland

"You may not realize it when it happens, but a kick in the teeth may be the best thing in the world for you."

– *Walt Disney*

I'll never forget the day I met Dan. It happened on the day of my arrival into the *"Therapeutic Community"* FRIENDS (Finding Recovery In Each New Day's Sunrise), a particularly memorable event for me. Flanked by guards I was escorted from the work camp building on the compound to the main facility, positioned in front of a door, and told to wait. A kid about my age opened the door a crack and squeezed through. He introduced himself as my mentor and told me what was about to happen in an attempt to cushion the shock. He then pushed opened the door and before I could even blink I was overwhelmed by a chorus of 50 singing inmates. They stood in two columns along each side of the door. As I walked in they all shook my hand, never missing a beat to their song. After I successfully navigated my way through the gauntlet they erupted with claps and cheers. They began chanting for a speech. I simply said that I was happy to be there, and I was. I knew this *"Therapeutic Community"* was the only thing standing between me and parole. They erupted in cheers and applause once more.

Then suddenly the mood in the room shifted palpably and there was silence. Rapidly, inmates began arranging chairs and a town crier of sorts notified everyone that there would be a *"Confrontation"* in five minutes. I was escorted to my room by my mentor and told that I didn't have to take part in what was about to occur. Curious, I responded that I might as well jump in with both feet. He seemed amused by this. After helping me put my things away he and I made our way back to the day-room.

The chairs had been set up in such a manner that the room resembled a small stadium or open theater, with the actors performing in the middle for everyone to see. Situated on the makeshift stage were 10 chairs: two sitting in opposition in the direct center with four chairs flanking either side. I took a seat near the back and watched as my mentor made his way to the center. I didn't know it then, but he was slated to be the Master of Ceremonies for the event. He wasted no time. After a few seconds he called Dan to the center of the room.

An unassuming, not quite middle aged man quietly took the seat and sat emotionlessly on his hands. Eight other inmates were quickly called up to participate in the *"Confrontation"*. As I listened a laundry list of offenses were read aloud. Dan had manipulated other inmates. Dan had manipulated the staff. He had lied, cheated, cussed, not bothered to tuck in his shirt, and even tinkled on the toilet seat without cleaning it up. He had been trading food and watching T.V when he wasn't allowed to. His attitude sucked and was getting worse by the day. And the greatest sacrilege: he hadn't been taking *"The Program"* seriously. It seemed to me that someone had been watching his every move and in fact someone had, fifty someones. When he finished, my mentor took the seat opposite from Dan and sat on his hands as well. Then he opened his mouth.

It started out cordial enough. But my mentor's voice rose quickly. Catching me off guard, he soon reached a deafening crescendo. He was screaming at Dan. He was cussing at Dan. Did Dan realize how much of a screw up he was? At this rate Dan would never complete *"The Program"*. Forget *"The Program"*, with this mentality Dan would never get out of prison period! How much of a disappointment to his family would that be? What would his children think when he was condemned to prison for life for refusing to tuck in his shirt or pissing on the toilet seat? Couldn't he see that he was on a path to Hell? Didn't he care?

I was the picture of shock and horror. This was not the way you spoke to other men in prison unless you wanted immediate violence. Yet I couldn't peel my eyes away from the spectacle. When the tears came, slowly at first, I could see that Dan was trying to hide them. But he was sitting on his hands. Soon tears were streaming down his face as one horrible image after another was forcefully impressed upon his mind by his fellow angry inmates. He began to shake and shudder. Snot began to flow freely. Shortly after that he was bawling openly. Still they came, one after another to the center chair for their opportunity to confront him. When they were finished volunteers were called up from the audience. Many answered the call. Frozen, I just stared. It was at that moment that I first saw the Program Director perched shrewdly in his chair. He was watching me, gauging my reaction. There was a slight smile playing on his lips. He was radiant with the glow of a man who has fulfilled his life's purpose and is enjoying every minute of it. Like a Potter-esqe Dementor, or a lizard in the sun, he sat there bathing in the despair, reveling in each heart-wrenching sob, pausing only to scribble on his clipboard or to take his eyes away from the ceremonial roast long enough to look at me. When it was over, and there was no one left to confront him, the Director stood and said some complimentary things about Dan, though he kept it brief. Then he allowed us to go outside. Three hours had elapsed. Almost unable to believe what I just witnessed, I followed as the other inmates led the way to the door outside, all the while questioning what I had gotten myself into.

"Power is not a means; it is an end. One does not establish a dictatorship in order to safeguard a revolution; one makes a revolution in order to establish the dictatorship. The object of persecution is persecution. The object of torture is torture. The object of power is power."

- George Orwell

The Un-crushable Human Spirit

"Outside" consisted of a small, well-worn track with an ancient weight pile to one side of it. The fence surrounding the compound was tall, intimidating, and covered top to bottom with razor wire. Being the shiny new toy in the group I was approached by a couple dozen inmates who wanted to welcome me to the program a little more personally, which was expected. I was polite, and after a few rounds of hand shaking and storytelling I managed to get enough personal space to make a few laps around the track by myself. The chance to be alone with my thoughts was a blessing. It felt like the shock was visibly radiating from my head. Ten or fifteen minutes had passed, though it seemed like 10 seconds, when I heard the sound of footsteps from behind working to catch up with me. I was in no mood for company and turned around to tell my newest would-be visitor exactly that but the words stopped short in my throat. It was Dan.

He had cleaned himself up pretty well. If one hadn't observed the shellacking he had just taken they would be inclined to think that this was just another normal day in the neighborhood. I waited for him to catch up.

"Shocking isn't it?" he asked when he had made the distance. He didn't bother introducing himself. No introduction was necessary.

I agreed that it was as he fell into step with me. We walked in silence for two full minutes. I noticed that he was walking perfectly upright and his head was held high, almost conscious of his posture. Gone were the guilt and shame I had witnessed. In their place was something I hadn't seen in quite a while. Not the faux-pride one witnesses so often in the prison environment, but real, authentic pride. The kind only accomplishing a major goal or surviving a serious tribulation can bring.

"It's all bullshit you know…" he said after a while, conspiratorially.

This surprised me. After the beating he had just taken at the hands of his fellow inmates I would've guessed that the last thing on his mind was confiding in anyone about *anything*, especially the new guy. How he could find humanity in anyone after that display was beyond my comprehension. I liked and admired him right away.

Our conversation could be accurately described as him venting and me listening, though it was much more than that. He was teaching me. I learned the unwritten rules of the program, crash-course style, just by listening to him that afternoon. I learned who was trustworthy and whom I needed to tread lightly around. Pettiness had the potential to ignite a forest fire in the *"Therapeutic Community"*. Dan had angered a single inmate and ended up with more than 10 attacking him by exposing his shortcomings to the staff. That one inmate was the same kid who greeted me at the door, my mentor. Certain behaviors were acceptable, others were not. Everyone had their clique but no one admitted it. Like a high school horror show it was a typical hierarchy with the seasoned inmates nearing release positioned at the top and the newbies like me at the very bottom. At the tip-top of the pyramid was the staff. Not the prison guard types I had grown accustomed to but social worker types who wore regular clothes, had long hair, and walked with a slouch. We were not allowed to speak to them directly outside of a group therapy session unless specifically designated to do so and designations rotated on a bi-weekly basis. If we had a concern we could write it down and run it up the chain of command. It would be answered eventually, if at all. Until then we could look forward to a nine month marathon of explosively emotional hours-long therapy sessions like the one we just endured, sprinkled with a much longer punitive deep cleaning of the day-room ten times a week. My comment was that it sounded like heaven on Earth. We both laughed. The guard on duty whistled, our signal to come inside. As we made our way to the door I caught sight of my mentor standing by the weight pile along with three or four of Dan's confronters. He was watching me very closely. They were all watching me.

One day a couple months later, as we were languishing in our collective cage, Dan suggested that I try my hand at selling cars when I got out. This seemed absurd to me at first as I had absolutely no experience doing such a thing and no real knowledge of cars. Besides, weren't car salesmen jobs reserved for creepy old men with sweater vests and horrible coffee breath? But the more I listened to him talk about it the more I was intrigued. There was good money in selling cars, he insisted, and absolutely no experience was necessary. The only thing you really needed was a pleasing personality. He seemed confident that I could easily make a living at it. Then he excused himself and stood up suddenly to take his leave as if he had forgotten something. It was a typical, though rare, two hour block of "Free-Time" for the *"Therapeutic Community"* and he and I were deeply involved in a game of chess, which he was winning. I took the opportunity to sit back from the board and survey the day-room.

With a few exceptions, 50 supposedly hardened criminals were all engaged in some form of childish diversion. Between the music videos, board games, dramatic phone antics, and even nap-time in the corner the casual observer might mistake this room full of prison inmates for a room full of kids if it weren't for all the stubble. I caught a glimpse of my mentor and his cohorts hovering over a Monopoly board. He and I had formed an alliance of sorts though I made it a point to avoid his clique. I could see that a few of them were just itching to catch me with my shirt un-tucked. So far they had been unsuccessful. In fact, aside from a few minor hiccups I was sailing smoothly along through the first couple months of *"The Program"*.

When Dan returned I could see that he had a photo album with him. Photos in prison are a deeply personal treasure and only shared with someone you would consider a friend, so I turned my attention away from the game. When he had located the page he was looking for he passed me the album.

The first few pictures featured an unimpressive looking

mountain of dirt. There were a few shots from different angles and I could tell that it was pretty big, but a mountain of dirt was all it seemed to be. I turned the page and saw a group of four young men with scraggly beards all standing at the base of the dirt mountain. Their teeth were shining through their beards in stark contrast to the dirt caking their skin and hair. Each one of them was smiling. There were close ups featuring each of the men and I could tell that one of them was a much younger Dan. Apart from the dirt, the defining feature of each person was the clear joy they were experiencing at that moment. I turned the page and smiled myself as I saw Dan staring back at me. This time the focus wasn't on him or the mountain but on what he was holding in his hands. Both of his hands were cupped together and overflowing with marble to golf ball-sized yellow rocks. Another photo showed all the men standing side by side, hands cupped and overflowing with shiny yellow rocks almost as bright as their smiles. The last photo was a close up of Dan. The rock in his hand was so big that it looked like an orange or a small grapefruit at first glance. By now though I was figuring out exactly what I was looking at. When I looked up from the album he was grinning slightly.

"Is that what I think it is?" I asked, almost unbelieving.

"It's gold." He said.

"And where's this?" I asked, pointing to a picture of the mountain.

"Brazil." He said simply.

"You worked in a Brazilian gold mine?" I asked, genuinely impressed.

"No, we owned it. The four of us here…" he said, pointing to the picture of the four smiling men. My eyes grew wide but not with disbelief. I was impressed.

"You own a gold mine?" I asked, incredulous.

"Not anymore. This picture is 20 years old. We exhausted this mine and then sold the land. But yes, I've mined for gold on several properties that I've owned. This mine was already built when we bought the land though." The grin had not left his lips. He was scouring the memory banks of his mind reminiscing about accomplishments I could only imagine. I couldn't deny my sudden pangs of jealousy.

"How did you come up with enough money to buy a gold mine?" I asked, unable to hide my amazement. My curiosity was really driving me now. I had to know how he did it.

"Selling cars." he said definitively, his smile growing wider. The young man from the photo was clearly visible now. He had made his point, and as I peppered him with questions concerning gold mining and car selling I couldn't help but detect a slight air of satisfaction. He was a salesman after all. He knew a done deal when he saw one.

Interview with a Salesman

Dan completed *"The Program"* and went home about six weeks later. By then he and I had forged a close friendship and he willingly shared with me everything he knew about the business of selling cars. Though my time passed a little slower as a result of his departure I was glad to see my friend go home. Four months later, with my own release days away, I made the decision to commit 100% to the goal of becoming a car salesman.

Upon my release I hit the pavement and submitted my resume all over town. The first call back for an interview came with a thrill of excitement and I made my way to the dealership with as much optimism as I could muster. When the interview ended poorly due to my criminal history, lack of experience or knowledge selling cars, and recent prison stint I told myself that it was no big deal. By the time the sixth interview ended on the same sour note however, I began to come to terms with the fact that I had a serious objection to overcome. I began to have feelings of dejection and doubt. There were moments when the possibility of my becoming a car salesman seemed like a hallucination. Then one day my grandmother approached me with an ad she had seen in the newspaper. It was published by a large new car dealership and it promised a bare minimum of $2500 per month as a wage for entry-level salespeople with special consideration given to those with absolutely no experience. I couldn't believe what I was reading. I pulled out my nicest dress clothes and prepared to drive to the dealership the following morning.

I almost turned around when I first saw it. There was no way I could hope for a position here. It was the nicest, cleanest building I had seen since my release. It was brand new and much more modern than any of the dealerships I had already been to. As I parked my car I could see that the salespeople were dressed more professionally than most of the managers I had already interviewed with. More importantly, there was a huge lot full of brand new vehicles that I knew nothing about. With my head high and my expectations low I reached for the large glass doors marking the entrance to the brightly lit showroom.

A pleasant, attractive young lady was sitting at a reception desk in the showroom. I could already see a couple of salesmen eyeing me with curiosity so I made my way toward her. I asked her for an application. She asked for my name and told me to wait in the lobby. This surprised me a little bit but I didn't protest. After a few minutes a different lady walked into the lobby and introduced herself to me as the Head of HR. I had never heard such a title before so I just smiled politely and shook her hand. She then explained that the application process for their dealership was a little different than what I might have already experienced. I was to fill out the entire application on a computer station set up specifically for that purpose. There would be an aptitude as well as a personality test administered. When I was finished I could simply pick up my things and leave. They would contact me for an interview if I made the cut. I let her know that I understood what was expected of me and sat down at the computer she had been directing me to.

I was surprised the next morning when she called before I even had time for breakfast. If I was available she had an opening at one to discuss the possibility of my becoming an employee. I tried not to sound too eager when I told her I would be there.

A little more confidently this time, I opened the large glass doors to the showroom. The receptionist smiled as I told her I had an appointment for one o'clock. She directed me to the lobby once more and I took a seat to wait. The Head of HR appeared, called my name, and waved me back to her office. As I sat down I could tell by the expression on her face that this was to be a serious meeting. She informed me that my test scores were excellent but that her real concern was the criminal history section. She had never seen one so completely filled out before. She would have to check with "corporate" to confirm that I was even eligible for employment. But before we got that far I would need to interview with the management, and that's what today was all about. If I was ready she would send them in now, one at a time. I told her that would be fine.

The first manager was young, tall, and slender. He spoke softly and went out of his way to be politically correct with his words. His one defining feature was his hair, which was a complete mess. He asked some preliminary questions about my experience in prison and the requirements of my parole, though he didn't seem to be interested in all the details. After some questions about my availability and whether or not I had reliable transportation he thanked me for my time and stood up to leave, telling me that the next manager would be in to speak with me in a minute.

I could tell before he even sat down that the second manager had been in the military. His hair was cropped short in a military crew cut and he walked perfectly upright with an unmistakable air of military bearing. He was no taller than me yet the seriousness of his demeanor was intimidating in and of itself. His ice blue eyes were hard and intelligent. He sat down without a smile and got straight to business. He wanted to know two basic questions: was I willing to do whatever they suggested to learn how to sell cars, and could I keep myself out of prison? Judging from my criminal history he frankly doubted the second one. Nervously I tried to assure him that I was a solid investment. I was on parole after all, and under strict supervision. Along with weekly group counseling sessions and random drug tests I was required to find and keep a job. I had just served two years and if I screwed up I could look forward to three more for my second helping. This seemed to assure him as it became obvious that there was indeed some sort of structure to my parole experience. After confirming that I had no problem being at work by 8:00 am he stood, extended his hand, and asked me to wait for the next manager.

The last manager had a calming air and personality. Slightly older than the previous two, and slightly heavier, his round jovial face had the familiarity of a favorite uncle you haven't seen in a few years. He smiled when he spoke and his maintenance of eye contact let whoever he was speaking to know that they were being listened to. He wasn't too concerned about my criminal history as he didn't ask a single question about it. He seemed more interested in my experience working at my grandparent's drive-in restaurant. After a few minutes of conversation in which he appeared to be gauging my personality more than anything he announced that I had made it through the interview process and he and the other managers were going to discuss the possibility of offering me a job. If I would wait in the lobby he would be out to talk to me in a few minutes. He smiled and extended his hand for me to shake and then he opened the door and led me back to the lobby. While I was waiting I passed the time chatting with one of the salesman. He was about my age and had been working there for a couple months. He loved his job, he said, and had an appointment later that day with a family looking to purchase a new Suburban. He was dressed much more nicely than I was. As I was admiring his cuff-links I caught sight of the third manager approaching me from the corner of my eye.

"We want you to talk to Steve. His office is over here." He said motioning for me to follow him.

Steve Smith, Sugar Daddies, the NFL, and the Mekong Delta

When Steve Smith was young he excelled at sports. As a kid he dabbled in most sports, as most of us do, but by high school he had decided to become a professional basketball player. Tall, lean, muscular, and most importantly quick, Steve was able to dominate all positions on the basketball court and after a few years of intense practice and determination he became the most valuable player on his high school team without exception. Simply because it was expected, and also because he enjoyed it so much, he played as quarterback on the football team as well. By his senior year he was attracting the attention of more than one college recruit and the future was looking bright indeed. When one of the recruits suggested he consider a career in football instead of basketball he laughed it off as a joke. He loved playing football and was a skillful quarterback but his passion was basketball. However, this particular recruiter was persistent and as a result Steve found himself being introduced to the world of *College-Football Sugar Daddies*.

You may or may not know that college football players are forbidden from receiving money in exchange for playing in games. On its surface this appears to make sense. But if I were to tell you that a cartel of decrepit, multi-millionaire fossils exists, that collects and benefits from every cent earned by college football while sharing absolutely nothing with the young players dedicating their bodies to the cause, you might reconsider your position. Regardless of how you might feel about the arrangement the free market has provided for the *College-Football Sugar Daddy,* and he has long been around to address the imbalance.

Sugar Daddies make sure that valuable college players and even entire universities receive any material item they might want outside of the restrictions of the NCAA and BCS cartels. Some *Sugar Daddies*, or *Boosters*, are tied to a particular university much more than a particular player/student and concentrate their efforts accordingly. This is done in a number of ways, most of them shielded from the view of the drunken tailgaters in the parking lot, all of them involving copious amounts of money and material possessions. Perhaps the most well known *Sugar Daddy* in the world is Phil Knight, the CEO of Nike. The teaser from a recent 2013 interview between Phil and the ultra-insider website www.thebeatofsports.com reads:

College Football's Ultimate Sugar Daddy

Oregon did not become a super power in college football overnight. But it now is one of the biggest brands in college athletics. It just opened its brand new $68 million football facility, barbershop and all. Sam Stites, editor-in-chief at the Daily Emerald, shares the story of the day Nike's Phil Knight and his fellow rich friends decided to make Oregon a major player in college football. Stites talks about the influence Knight has on the school and what Knight's critics are saying. Plus, he answers the question of what brand of sneakers he wears.

– www.thebeatofsports.com August 1ˢᵗ, 2013

After some serious consideration Steve decided to become a football player. During his college tenure his financial needs were seen to by a (strictly platonic) *Sugar Daddy,* and as a result he was able to concentrate on developing himself into the best quarterback he could possibly become. He was drafted into the NFL by a Midwestern team upon graduation and though not granted a starting position, he was immediately assigned to the backup quarterback position. The future had never shined brighter. And then war broke out. Three months into his tenure as a professional football player Steve was drafted again, this time by the Marines as The United States of America declared war on Vietnam. For Steve the next life changing decision wasn't even much of a challenge. It was done out of a sense of obligation more than anything. Steve Smith, 23 year old homegrown patriot and recent NFL draftee, headed off to boot camp.

Steve served two tours in Vietnam. His speed, strength, endurance, intelligence and ability secured him a position on the special operations unit where he would routinely lie in wait for more than a week in one rice paddy or another until his target was unfortunate enough to cross his path. The first time he killed a man it affected him terribly. By the tenth time he did it, it had become a difficult, though bearable routine. After finishing his service Steve came home to America. Because his expenses had been paid by the U.S. Military during his service (and because he had been an astute saver all of his life, including his NFL and military pay) a rather large bank account was waiting for him. After learning the *Art of Selling*, and working for a few years as both a salesman and a manager, Steve purchased a Ford dealership in Michigan. For the next 20 years he skillfully grew the business into the sales leader of the region. By the time he decided to retire and sell the dealership Steve Smith had achieved *Financial Independence* many times over. He built a magnificent house on a beautiful piece of Rocky Mountain property and set about the machinations of retirement with his wife by his side. For a few years he kept himself busy cultivating the land around his property. But as time wore on Steve grew restless. When the opportunity to turn around a sub-par dealership in Caldwell, Idaho presented itself he leapt at it. You can only do so much landscaping and tree planting after all. He was hired as the General Manager, with the goal of turning the dealership around and given enormous leeway with his hiring/firing decisions, which for me was nothing less than a blessing.

The 20 Club

Of course I was completely ignorant of his history as I took the seat opposite from Steve in the General Managers office that day. From my perspective he was nothing more than a distinguished looking older man. He greeted me with a handshake and then sat down and directed his attention to my application. On the wall behind him was a wide angle lens style poster of Vince Lombardi, a man I had never heard of. A golden football sat on the desk behind him. After reading over my application for a full 30 seconds he lifted his head to speak. Instead his eyebrows rose questioningly.

"So is that the new style or something?" he asked. He was looking at my neckline. Instinctively my hand shot to my throat. In my haste I had forgotten to button the top of my dress shirt. My tie and neckline were an exposed, sloppy mess; an excellent first impression. Already I felt my chances diminishing. As I went through the motions of putting myself back together I wondered why the other managers hadn't brought it to my attention.

Naturally, the first thing we discussed was my time in prison. He too seemed comforted by the fact that I was being strictly supervised on parole. He appeared satisfied when I explained that my obsession for money had driven me to do some stupid things and that my time in prison had forced me to accept that I was the only person to blame for my choices. If he would allow me the opportunity I would love to focus my attention on more socially acceptable forms of wealth gathering, such as selling cars. He let it go at that and turned his attention back to my application. Then his eyes rose skeptically,

"It says here that you speak Spanish…?" He asked looking

straight into my eyes.

"I read and write it as well." was my reply.

Without hesitating he picked up his phone and punched a button. Though he spoke quietly his voice boomed over the intercom, "Miguel to Steve's office, please."

A well dressed Hispanic man entered the office a few seconds later. He was one of the salesmen I had seen upon my arrival. "How can I help you Steve?" he said as shut the door behind him.

"This kid says he can speak Spanish." He said, looking at Miguel but nodding toward me.

Miguel turned to me, "Oh yeah? So where'd you learn it?"

My transition was flawless, "School, but I have a few friends who speak as well."

"High School?"

"No, college. I was studying to become a teacher and then I caught a couple felonies and ended up in prison for two years."

"And now you want to sell cars?"

"Well, a friend of mine told me there was good money in it."

"He's right you know. Where are you from?"

"I was born in Nampa, but I grew up in Boise."

"How long have you been speaking Spanish?"

"Almost four years."

With that he turned to Steve. "It sounds like it to me." He said.

"Thanks Miguel, that's all." Steve said. Miguel nodded farewell and made his exit. I watched him walk through the door and then turned my eyes back to Steve. He was looking at me with what seemed to be honest surprise, his head slightly tilted and his mouth slightly open. Any doubt or skepticism of my claims to bilingual ability had just been erased from his mind.

"Can you pass a drug test?" he asked seriously.

"Of course." I replied.

"I'll have to pull some strings with corporate because of your record. But if everything works out, and I think it will, I'd like to offer you a job." He said. My face lit up. I could barely contain my excitement. "We'll give you a call to confirm, but can you be here by 8:00 am Monday morning?"

"Absolutely!" I said, a little too enthusiastically.

"And when I say eight, I mean eight Lombardi Time. Do you know what that means?"

"I don't." I confessed. I sheepishly glanced back up at the picture of Vince on the wall.

"It means be here at 7:45."

Under the tutelage of Steve and the other managers (and even a couple of salesmen) I learned the *Art of Selling*. During the first few weeks on the sales floor most salespeople are expected to "shadow" another salesperson in an attempt to learn the ropes. After the first two car deals however my shadowing experience was over. I simply did not want to split the commission anymore (which is what occurs when two salespeople are involved in a deal). Because our dealership had an open floor policy, and because I noticed that about half of the sales force seemed solely concerned with how much coffee they could drink on the showroom floor while sitting on their ass, I put on my heavy coat and made the crowded car lot my new stomping grounds. I was rewarded for this many times in the form of car deals that wouldn't have existed had it not been for a salesman being in the right place at the right time. The right place being in between the customer and the car they want to buy. The right time being whenever they chose to show up.

By the time "The Hammer" made his appearance I was on a roll. Winter had given way to summer and I was looking forward to my fifth month as a car salesman. During my fourth month I sold 16 cars and earned the largest paycheck I had ever earned in my life. I remember being amused when at the morning sales meeting during the first day of the new month the sales managers were a little more excited than usual. They made it known that a new salesman had just been hired; a rugged, experienced, junkyard dog type who had been-there-and-done-that. Therefore, we had all better be on our toes. Almost on cue a large, loud man entered the sales bullpen. His aura of arrogance was palpable, the line between it and his confidence clearly crossed long ago. He surveyed the bullpen, gave a smug little snort, and then introduced himself in the following way:

"If any of you guys have any trouble gettin' your customer closed just turn 'em over to 'The Hammer' and I'll get 'em done for ya! So where's my desk?" I rolled my eyes while stifling a gag.

But by the end of the day, after "The Hammer" had cracked out two fresh car deals, I was compelled to pay closer attention to his presence. I wouldn't have bought a breakfast burrito from this guy but he had managed to sell two fresh ups on his first day! Naturally, the sales staff was ablaze with indignant and skeptical chatter. With the exception of Steve the management team could only be described as giddy with delight. An eager sales manager wondered aloud if "The Hammer" was what they had all been waiting for. Another suggested that "The Hammer" be given a free pass on the company-mandated two week training period, as he obviously didn't need it. Shocked, I was confronted by the fact that if I didn't step up my game this large, bellicose new salesman would eat the lunch right off my plate as I sat staring at it. Looking back, with all the benefit that hindsight provides, I can safely say that was the day I decided to join *The 20 Club*.

The 20 Club was the moniker given to an exclusive group of salesmen who had sold at least 20 cars in any given calendar month. Not one of the current sales staff was a member. Every two weeks, which is how often most car salesman sign a new pay plan, I was reminded of the existence of *The 20 Club* by being forced to acknowledge the amazing incentive involved: a one thousand dollar cash bonus and a ¼ carat diamond ring. Occasionally, one of the seasoned salesmen on the floor would bring up the most recent recipient of the coveted *20 Club* ring, usually right after escorting one of their former customers to whatever manager they demanded to speak to. That particular salesman had left the dealership a few months before I was hired and, if the steady stream of his former customers were to be believed, was a notorious liar. Every stereotype of a sleazy salesman you've ever heard in your life could supposedly be attributed to this character, and accurately. I suspected that the same could be true for my current nemesis. My determination to succeed became that much more solidified.

As the month progressed "The Hammer" and I were neck

and neck in terms of the sales leader board. Halfway through the month I had delivered 13 cars and the prospect of joining *The 20 Club* was becoming more real to me by the day. Then "The Hammer" caught his second wind. He delivered his 20th car deal with one day to spare before the month's end. Strutting and preening on the sales floor shortly afterwards he informed those of us who would listen that he was taking the last day of the month off to enjoy a well deserved drink. The scene in the sales office was nothing short of hilarious. Steve was vainly attempting to convince one of his three star struck sales managers that the dancing peacock they were watching through the window was nothing but a flash in the pan. This made me feel better. Though with one day left, 19 cars delivered, and not a single prospect on my immediate calendar, I realized that my goal was quickly slipping from my grasp.

I was scheduled to come in at noon the following day. I showed up at 8:00 am. After working the phone and pounding the lot into the evening I still had not discovered a customer who was ready to buy. With an hour to go before closing time most of the salesmen were picking up their desks and preparing to call it a weekend. I was beginning to feel real discouragement. Standing on the lot, looking down at my phone and lamenting the fact that I had come within a single car deal of my goal while being one-upped by the most odious competition imaginable, I contemplated how I would nurse my wounded ego back to health. I barely noticed as a car pulled in the far entrance. Defeated, I made no attempt to pursue it. Most people pulling in the far entrance were simply looking to turn around anyway. But then, after about 30 seconds of closely scrutinizing the Cobalts, the buyer spotted me, the unsuspecting, apathetic salesman staring dumbly at his phone. He zoomed toward me and pulled up to the curb I was standing on.

"Do you speak Spanish?" he asked in his native tongue.

"Occasionally, when it pays." I replied smiling, looking up. He smiled back. He was younger than I was and sitting next to him in the passenger seat was his young wife.

"I'm looking for a black Cobalt SS. You got anything like that?" he asked very straightforwardly.

"Actually I do," was my astonished reply, "it just came in today." And it had, though my heart sank. This was a thirty thousand dollar car this twenty-something and I were discussing, and it was the furthest thing from black.

Earlier, while stomping around the lot searching for a car deal, I watched as the delivery truck dropped off about fifteen vehicles, a common occurrence at most moving and shaking dealerships. One vehicle in particular was sticking out like a sore thumb. It was the bright yellow paint and the obnoxious spoiler that first caught my eye. I recognized immediately that we had just received our first Chevrolet Cobalt SS. It was rushed through the Pre-Delivery inspection process that very afternoon and was currently sitting next to the detail garage awaiting its first bath. It still had the factory applied shrink-wrap and foam padding on its doors. The darkened garage windows told me that our detail guy had already snuck away for the weekend. My prospective customer parked his car and disembarked with his wife. I realized that they weren't just looking, they were shopping. I greeted them and then cautiously walked them over toward the bright yellow car.

As we walked I held two conversations, one with my customer and one with myself. Qualifying a customer politely can be difficult, but any salesperson worth their salt must learn to finesse the skill into an art form, or better yet, a simple conversation. With this particular customer the conversation was immediately encouraging. The other "conversation" could more accurately be described as a screaming match, and it was occurring nowhere except within my own head. Phantom objections, invented entirely by a petrified salesperson, are easily their own worst enemy, something I had become familiar with despite my success. Almost like a mental racquetball match, every objection I had heard up to that point was firing off rapidly in my mind and just as quickly I was swatting them away, which was my unique way of dealing with my own fears. I noticed that my customer fell silent as the car came into our view.

He said nothing about the color as we approached the car. Neither did I. Stealthily, I removed the key from the lockbox and activated the remote start. The engine roared to life with a satisfying growl. Popping the hood, trunk, and both doors for my customers (mercifully the interior was sleek, black leather) I preformed a silent walk around, running my hand lightly along the perfect body lines, softly caressing the spoiler with my fingers. The sun was halfway below the horizon and there was still enough light that I could barely gauge my new customer's facial reactions. They were very encouraging.

"Are you guys closing up for the night?" he asked, his eyes glued to the car.

"No," I lied easily, "I'm still here for another hour." Silently we circled the car once more. I noticed more than a couple excited glances pass between husband and wife.

"I know it's getting late, but can we take it for a ride?" he asked sincerely.

"Absolutely." was my excited, measured reply.

One ride was all it took to seal that deal. By the time I had translated the financial paperwork involved for my new customers it was well past eleven. I thought about accepting the invitation to go out and celebrate with the two of my co-workers who remained, but turned it down. I was scheduled to be in at eight the next morning and I was exhausted. Feeling the full satisfaction that only comes with successfully completing a major goal I headed home and went to bed.

When I arrived to work the next morning Steve was filling out the sales board with statistics from the previous month. He was just finishing and I noticed that he had changed my final tally to 21 instead of 20.

"What's the 21 all about?" I asked anyone in general.

One of the managers answered me, "Steve can't stand that 'The Hammer' stole your limelight so we're going to tell him you knocked out 21 for the month, okay?" Steve was filling in an arbitrary number on the board. His back was turned to us but I could almost feel him smiling at the thought of selling "The Hammer" a lie such as this.

"Okay," I agreed, and made my way to the bullpen to prepare for Steve's morning sales meeting.

As things would turn out "The Hammer" barely noticed. Scheduled to work at the same time as the rest of us on a morning shift barely two weeks later, "The Hammer" was conspicuously absent at the 8:30 am sales meeting. Calls to his cell phone went unanswered. Excuses were floated around the room by a sympathetic manager or two. When he waltzed in after noon, wearing shorts and a Hawaiian shirt, announcing that he was quitting effective immediately and demanding his paycheck, I could have sworn that I saw a slight smile of satisfaction playing on the corner of Steve's mouth. This was obviously not the first flash in the pan he had called. Pleas from the other managers to reconsider fell on deaf ears as I watched Steve and "The Hammer" make their way to the accounting office to sign whatever paperwork was necessary. As quickly as he had arrived, "The Hammer" was gone.

Winds of Change

Nature's first green is gold,
Her hardest hue to hold.
Her early leaf's a flower;
But only so an hour.
Then leaf subsides to leaf.
So Eden sank to grief,
So dawn goes down to day.
Nothing gold can stay.

"Nothing Gold Can Stay" – Robert Frost

2006 was an amazing year for me, one full of accomplished goals and lessons learned. When things began to change (as things tend to do) I was admittedly not ready for it. A month into the new year Steve was given a promotion to a multi-store manager position and announced that he would be leaving us as our General Manager. Some cheered the move but I was devastated. The next GM and I would experience a tenuous, tension-filled relationship as our industry began to feel the first tremors of the financial collapse to come full force in 2008. Nine months into his tenure he was replaced by yet another GM, this one nothing short of psychotic, who I would labor under for another year. But after three years the cohesiveness of our little dealership had all but deteriorated. When what should have been an easy car deal devolved into a hysterical, customer-scaring screaming match in the sales office between the GM and myself (one which resulted in me being contacted by the Corporate Office, demanding to know if I had been "harassed"…) I knew that it was time for me to take a calculated risk.

That risk, quitting my job and attempting the creation of a small business, was the hardest part. Not the act of quitting per-se but rather the mental gymnastics involved in coming to a determined decision. And not because I loved my job so much (though for the first year I really did) but because I knew that my income was likely to take a dramatic hit during the first couple years, which it did.

Thinking back to the day I quit my job as a car salesman always brings me some measure of amusement. I arrived for my shift fifteen minutes early (cheers Vince!) and simply announced my decision to quit. It was effective immediately, of course, as there is no such thing as a two week notice for car salesmen. With one exception the management team was taken by surprise, which they hate. Later, one of my fellow salesman told me all about the angry tongue lashing that everyone who admitted to knowing about my plan received when the General Manager deemed it acceptable to throw a fit in that day's sales meeting. Hearing this surprised me because he was cordial enough to my face. He asked me very directly what had caused me to make my decision and upon hearing my answer almost barked out laughing,

"You're throwing away a fifty thousand dollar per year job for a snow cone shack!?" He was barely able to hide his surprise, or his contempt.

I assured him that I was. He wished me luck and dismissed me with a quick, formal shake of his hand. I went to the accounting office and picked up my final check which, conveniently, was both more than I expected and issued immediately. I slid out the back door while the aforementioned sales meeting was probably just getting started and was surprised to see a friend, the one manager who knew of my plan and said nothing, waiting for me in the parking lot. He was standing next to my car with a cigarette in his hands, a look of slight disbelief on his face. Maybe it was slight envy. We talked for a while and his wishes of good luck were sincere. It was he who had most enthusiastically encouraged and supported the idea of me going into business for myself though he had always suggested a coffee shop. He was full of so many good ideas that I would later use. I thanked him for everything he had done to help me over the past three years and jumped in my car, a beautiful green Cadillac that three years previously I could have only fantasized about driving. I pulled away from the dealership for the millionth and last time, the sun shining in my face, the open road ahead of me the only object of my focus.

4

Hawaiian Shave Ice, a crash course

When I tell people what I do for a living I'm usually asked some variable of the following question: *What gave you the idea to open a Shaved Ice shack?*

The answer is that I didn't plan to open up a *Shaved Ice* shack. My plan was to open a drive-through coffee business. But after researching the idea I discovered that, among other obstacles, it would have taken far more startup capital than I was able to come up with.

I began to entertain the idea of going into business for myself about three months after Steve left the dealership. The second General Manager was a tyrant and in moments of tension my mind would wander to fantasies of telling him off and quitting on the spot. I figured that it would be easy to put myself out there to different dealerships considering my newfound experience and success, and it probably would have been. But one of the sales managers, and someone I consider a friend, had a different idea. A big coffee drinker, he suggested I open a drive-through coffee business.

The idea piqued my interest and I began my due diligence into the matter. I started with city government offices to check which regulations governed the business. Each "Department" has its own regulations to abide by and licensing fees to collect. Because there were plenty of existing coffee shops for sale I sought out current owners and asked them as many questions as they were willing to answer. Most of them were willing to share at least a little information. Some were openly hostile, which you must be prepared for. Some people desire to share nothing at all about their business, especially with a prospective competitor, and that is absolutely their right.

As I did my homework three major obstacles became apparent to me. First, big names like Starbucks, Moxie Java, and Dutch Bros. had long ago gobbled up the lion's share of the coffee market and put more than a few shop owners out of business by offering a superior product, in a better environment, for a comparable price. This left the independent coffee vendors competing against each other for the small percentage of remaining customers and working long hours just to keep their enterprise afloat. Second, there were simply too many independent coffee vendors over-populating their share of the market. It seemed like every corner gas station had a drive through coffee stand in the parking lot, each doing just enough business to get by. The third obstacle was the profitability of coffee in general. The price of coffee was reaching new highs with each passing day putting the squeeze on already paper-thin profit margins. I began to realize that if I wanted my venture into business ownership to succeed I would have to find something to sell besides coffee.

This realization was a process and something I thought about daily as I drove back and forth to my job as a car salesman. As summer approached that year I noticed a *Shaved Ice* shack pop up in a parking lot about a mile away from the dealership. Every time I drove by it I thought, *"That's a terrible spot for a shack! If it were mine I would put it here…"* As this went on it slowly dawned on me that the idea I had been looking for was right under my nose the entire time.

The Difference Between Snow Cones and Shaved Ice

Shaved Ice Specific Tip #1 – *Use a real ice shaver to sell real Shaved Ice and always sell the best product you can get your hands on.*

Stop and think for a minute. What separates a company like Starbucks from a locally owned, independent coffee stand in the minds of many consumers? If you answered, *"They offer a superior product"* you might be correct. If you answered, *"They have Brand Recognition"* you would definitely be correct, but we'll get to that shortly. For now let's focus on the quality of the product. It hardly matters whether its coffee shops, restaurants, or clothing stores, we're comparing. The regulars who frequent these establishments will tell you almost every time that the *consistent quality* of the product offered is what brings them back.

It might surprise you to learn that there are frauds and perpetrators in the *Shaved Ice* business. These phonies tend to be guided by the same shoddy principles. Armed with a few cheap *Shaved Ice* banners and some horrible tasting generic syrup they have been known to set up shop using any manner of janky crushed ice machine they can buy for a hundred dollars and then try to pass off the resulting excrement as *Shaved Ice*. This is a huge faux-paus if you want to be successful in this business and, trust me here, your customers will know if you attempt such chicanery. *Shaved Ice* does not come from ice cubes. It is not crushed in a machine. It does not come from a rectangular block of ice that you buy at the grocery store. It comes from a cylindrical block of ice that you freeze yourself which is spun over a super-sharp Japanese blade. A word about filtering your water should be offered here. If you're not filtering what you mistakenly believe to be contaminant-free water, you should try it. In my opinion filtered water makes not only for a cleaner block of ice but a fluffier, better tasting finished product.

So what brand of machine do I recommend? To my knowledge there are only two proper manufacturers of authentic *Shaved Ice* machines, Swan and Hatsayuki. Both are made in Japan and both of their nearly identical machines are the only NSF certified machines on the market today. Both are equally suitable for creating the best *Shaved Ice* possible. While I won't go so far as to label anything else a generic imposter, I will stress that these are the only two brands of machine I personally recommend.

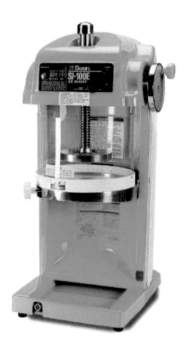

A Swan Shaved Ice machine   *A Hatsuyuki Ice Shaver.*

A Snow Cone machine

*Shaved Ice **does not** shoot into a cup at the pull of a lever.*

Speaking of imposters, in the time I've been selling *Shaved Ice* I've heard the product called every name under the sun: Freezie, Icee, Snow Cone, Slushie, Sno Ball, even Water Ice (which is an east coast thing and the furthest thing from *Shaved Ice*).

Hawaiian Shave Ice, as it's properly called, doesn't come from Hawaii. It actually originated in Japan over a thousand years ago. During an epoch in their history referred to as the *Heian Period* Japanese royalty and the wealthy 1% of the day would send their servants to the mountains to collect ice which was then shaved and topped with fruit or sweet beans. They called this mixture *Kakigori* and it is hugely popular in Japan to this day. The practice was brought to Hawaii by migrant Japanese sugar plantation workers during the 19th century where it would eventually morph into the Americanized version that most of us know and love. Traditionally it is served with fruit, beans, green tea, condensed milk, cream or even ice cream in addition to syrup depending on your location as *Shaved Ice* is recognized the world over, but especially in Asia. In Korea it's called *Patbingsu.* In China it's referred to as *Baobing* and in Taiwan it's called *Xue Hua Bing.* In Mexico they call it *Raspas* or *Raspados.* In Boise, Idaho (where I proudly live) *Hawaiian Shave Ice* is usually referred to as *Shaved Ice* or simply, snow cones.

Green Tea flavored Japanese Kakigori. With a little style.

Kurokuma is a type of Kakigori. It is derived from Shirokuma.

Korean Patbingsu with fruit and ice cream.

A plate of Chinese Bao Bing with strawberries and condensed milk.

Taiwanese Xue Hua Bing

Mexican Raspas

A Mexican Raspado in Colonia Doctores, Mexico City.

Traditional Hawaiian Shaved Ice

President Barack Obama is known to be a fan of Shaved Ice.

How to Start a Shaved Ice Shack

Step #1 – *Make contact with a quality manufacturer and establish a relationship with them.*

In my opinion, the one *Shaved Ice* product that offers both *Superior Quality* **and** *Brand Recognition* is manufactured by Tropical Sno. I have personally tried many different syrups manufactured by many different companies. I prefer Tropical Sno by a wide margin. That is why I've built my business around it. That is why I recommend it exclusively always keeping in mind *Shaved Ice Specific Tip #1.*

I understand that not everyone will adhere to my strict standards (after all taste is relative) but I would be derelict in my duty if I advised you to use any other syrup than that which is manufactured by Tropical Sno because I believe their quality is unparalleled. I also understand that they are not the cheapest syrup available, nor do they offer every conceivable flavor. At the end of the day you can only buy what is in the best interest of you and your business which is solely for you to decide. But before you commit to any other product ask yourself the following: Does the product I'm considering offer *Protected Territory?* Any brand name worth mentioning will offer dealers of their product *Protected Territory.* This means that a certain area around your business (typically a square mile or two) is protected from other would-be dealers of the same product (though not from competition). Am I able to sample the product I'm considering before I commit to signing an agreement to become an exclusive dealer of it? Often, a manufacturer will offer to send you a sample of one or two of their flavors as an incentive to try their product and consider offering it over the competition. This is a bold statement, the equivalent of daring you to compare, and something I recommend that you always take advantage of. Am I doing business with (and representing) a company that will make sure I have a point man I can contact any time I have a concern, someone qualified to help me in my endeavor? Are there tangible examples of other people who have achieved success peddling the same product I'm considering? The brand I'm recommending is recognized world-wide and has a friendly, helpful staff available to assist you year round.

"Just" Desserts

I can't tell you how many times I've heard some variation of the following claims, usually coughed up by someone with little to zero experience selling *Shaved Ice*:

- *"It's just sugar and water, these kids can't tell the difference..."*

- *"Kids aren't concerned with quality. They just want something sweet and cold on a hot day..."*

- *"I can save X-Amount of dollars if I go with Brand-X. I just can't afford to go with anything else..."*

Personally, I'm of the opinion that if you really feel this way about your customers then you deserve to fail. Believing that you can start a business and become successful by offering your customers an inferior product is like believing you can blindly throw a thousand dollars at the *"Stock Market"* and become a millionaire. It will never happen. More importantly, if you're serious about succeeding why would you consider offering anything but the best product to your customers? Keep in mind that children are not the exclusive consumer of *Shaved Ice*. Many adults love the unique product and if the time is taken to prepare it properly they will return regularly to your establishment, providing you with more income over time than you ever thought possible from one person. It should go without saying that this is how you build a successful business: one satisfied customer at a time.

Step #2 – *Procure a building, vendors cart, or enclosed mobile unit.*

    If you aren't capable of constructing your own building from the ground up you will either have to pay someone to do it for you or buy a prefabricated building. There are many commercial mobile and semi-mobile vending units available for sale at any given time and I highly recommend going in that direction if you can afford it. If you are not able to find a reasonably priced commercial mobile unit I would recommend paying someone to construct a *Semi-Permanent*, movable, kiosk-type building for you or convert a prefabricated shed into a building fit to do business. This can usually be done for much cheaper than the cost of purchasing a commercial mobile vending unit. As of the time of this writing, converting a prefabricated shed into a building fit for business can be done for five to seven thousand dollars, sparing no expense. Remember to add skids made of treated wood to the underside of your building to facilitate moving it. Keep in mind that unless you have access to a winch, truck, and a flatbed trailer you will need to arrange to have your building moved from place to place. This can typically be done by professional shed movers for a few hundred dollars per move.

Step #3 – *Procure a real Shaved Ice machine and learn how to use it.*

This is important so it bears repeating: the only authentic *Shaved Ice* machines that I know of are manufactured by Swan and Hatsayuki, both Japanese companies. You use anything else at your own peril. As you might have guessed these machines are not cheap. Not many industrial-grade machines are. I have spoken with many would-be success stories who mistakenly thought they might get away with purchasing a three hundred dollar knock-off machine only to be frustrated with both the product produced and the cheapness/unreliability of the machine itself. My advice is that you always buy a Swan or Hatsayuki machine. If the price tag on a new unit makes you queasy check Craigslist, eBay, Amazon or some similar marketplace. I have purchased a few lightly used machines from former business owners, serviced them myself, and marveled as they produced their purchase price in terms of product sold in as little as three days.

Anatomy of a Good Location

Step #4 – *Scout out a Good Location and negotiate a favorable lease.*

Hyde Park, last day of the season

A *Good Location* is the single most important factor that will determine whether your enterprise will be an amazing success story or a dramatic failure. However, a *Good Location* could potentially only be as good as the lease you're able to negotiate. I understand that real estate values (and therefore rent rates) are different depending on where you are located, but in general you don't want to commit to more than a few hundred dollars in rent per month. Also, it is not unreasonable to ask for the landlord to include the cost of electricity in the lease though don't let that be a deal breaker. *Shaved Ice* businesses use a minimal amount of electricity and can be operated at a very small cost in comparison to other small, enclosed businesses like coffee shacks.

The overall goal in establishing a successful *Good Location* should be insane profitability. One of the quickest ways to ruin the formula I'm prescribing is to commit to paying more rent than you otherwise could have if you only would have been a little savvier during the negotiation phase. Keep in mind that there is absolutely no reason to rush into any location. Ask yourself if the location you're considering meets the following criteria. Only then can you have an educated idea of its value.

Plainly speaking a *Good Location* has **all** of the following:

1. Close proximity to one or more neighborhood and/or schools.
2. Close proximity to an additional attraction such as a swimming pool, park/sports field, or gas station/restaurant/movie theater which is frequented by people looking to spend money.
3. Heavy walkup foot traffic.
4. Comfortable seating, usually well shaded, for customers to enjoy/provide free advertising.
5. Amazing visibility.

There are other factors that figure into the location equation. There are also some exceptions. Do you accept credit/debit cards? If you haven't heard of Square you need to educate yourself about their products and services as soon as possible. Are you set up to accept food stamps/EBT cards? Do you have internet access? Internet access, even through your phone, can be an important tool in helping you cheaply and quickly process credit/debit card orders. It also helps to alleviate boredom during the inevitable down-time you will experience. Do you offer a punch card that rewards customer loyalty? Is there a gimmick you're not exploiting properly that could drive an increase in sales (adding something cheap and small for example, such as a gummi-worm, at no added cost to the customer)? Do you offer cream topping or condensed milk? How about a scoop of ice cream at the bottom of the cup? This is an excellent way to increase profitability. Adding dairy products will step up your risk/inspection level with the health department, but that doesn't mean it can't be done. Finally, is there a restroom (preferably a clean one with a hand washing sink) nearby that your employee can utilize if they need to? After all, you never know when nature might come calling.

Now is an appropriate time to offer a word of advice about drive-by and drive-through traffic. While you're scouting potential locations for that elusive all-around winner you might be tempted by an otherwise questionable spot because of the number of cars driving by it on a daily basis. Avoid this pitfall. Drive-by/drive-through traffic is great for fast food and coffee sales but usually adds little benefit to *Shaved Ice* businesses apart from visibility. *Shaved Ice* is not something you can wolf down while driving. The person eating it will often create a little bit of a mess. Even the most experienced *Shaved Ice* connassoir knows this. That's why they prefer to sit down while they eat it. I'm not trying to suggest that drive-by/drive-through traffic is ineffective and shouldn't be considered at all. I'm simply saying that if a particular location you've been scouting has excellent drive-by traffic but is otherwise questionable you probably want to keep looking.

Step #5 – *Get your permits in line and place your building.*

Depending on where you live this step will come with varying degrees of difficulty. Some communities are very vendor friendly while some are not. Typically a *Shaved Ice* business is classified along the lines of a Temporary Vendor/Street Peddler and requires accompanying permits. Some communities will insist you speak with a number of different departments. Others will handle everything competently within one department, sometimes with one person, which is the most desirable position to be in. The bottom line is that you don't want to make the mistake of setting up your business without getting the proper permits in place. It will be a costly mistake that you will surely regret. Besides, it's really not that difficult. If I can do it so can you.

Because *Shaved Ice* does not contain dairy it is designated "Low Risk" by the local Health Department where I live. This means that *Shaved Ice* businesses are not subject to annual Health Department inspections. However, *Shaved Ice* is often served with cream topping. Tropical Sno offers a non-dairy cream topping that is wildly popular, tastes amazing, and boosts your profits. Be sure to check with your local Health Department for the regulations governing dairy products where you live before offering *anything* containing dairy.

Keep It Simple

When I was a kid one of my favorite summer hangouts was the public swimming pool. Located in the park by the Jr. High School about a mile away from my house, the public pool offered three of my favorite activities of the era: swimming, chasing girls, and snow cones.

The Snow Shack, as we called it, was a staple of the public pool. Even now as look into the past I can see the long line of eager children, dollars folded in their wet little hands, waiting in line at the Snow Shack. If you look close enough there in the middle you can see my brother and me, nine and ten years old respectively, waiting along with the crowd for our turn at the window. Our only concern was whether or not we would make it to the window before they ran out of our favorite flavors which happened more often than not due to the seemingly never-ending line of thirsty kids.

The idea was so simple, and yet had eluded me for so long, that when it finally took root and began to grow I was embarrassed I hadn't thought of it earlier. At work the Reign of the Third General Manager had just begun and I was more determined than ever to separate myself from what were becoming the shackles of employment. I made the decision that I would open my first *Shaved Ice* location while I was still employed, foolishly telling myself that I could manage both of the responsibilities at the same time. I purchased a building and outfitted it with the help of my carpenter best friend (which everyone should be lucky enough to have). Because of my childhood experience at the public pool I skipped the learning curve so often involved in determining the *highest quality product*. I contacted Tropical Sno seeking information from the company on getting involved in the business and was referred to Ron and Darlene who have been my patient and gracious mentors ever since. I shared my plan with them, including my proposed location, which Darlene wasn't excited about. She reckoned I could do much better setting up in a different part of town, which leads me to:

Shaved Ice Specific Tip #2 – *Stick to your Definite Major Purpose.*

And…

Shaved Ice Specific Tip #3 – *Seek out an accomplished mentor and follow their advice.*

I'm as confident, independent, and stubborn as they come. Because of this I forged ahead with my original plan without regard for the wise advice I received in the process that would have helped me immensely. Fortunately, I learned from this experience and only made that mistake my first year. The location I was hell-bent on establishing turned out to be much less successful than I had envisioned and I was unable to properly manage it due to my responsibilities at work. This experience compelled me to re-examine my Definite Major Purpose, becoming *Financially Independent*, in a new light. I was finally beginning to understand that if I was to become successful I would need to open my mind and become receptive to the advice, suggestions, and help of others, *especially* when they were superior to my own ideas.

This was also when I definitely decided to quit my job, though I knew I would have to conceal my intentions and wait for exactly the right time to do it. I feel that a word about multi-tasking should be offered here. Personally, I didn't achieve *Financial Independence* until I quit my job thereby forsaking the Definite Major Purpose of my employer for my own. However, I'm not trying to suggest that multi-tasking in this regard (that is, holding two jobs or even two careers) can't be done successfully. I *am* trying to suggest though that if you're not a professional with an optimal employment schedule (for example, a school teacher with no summer school commitments) your journey will be difficult, perhaps more difficult than it needs to be.

To Franchise, or not to Franchise…

When performing your due diligence on different *Shaved Ice* companies and the products they offer you might be confronted by the idea of *Franchising*. I highly recommend *Franchising* if one, you have a lot of money, and two, you're looking into nationally recognized brands of fast food with proven business models and protected territories (think McDonalds, Taco Bell, ect...). *Franchising* can be a very profitable idea for the tradesman/entrepreneur as well (think Jiffy Lube, Merry Maids, Meineke, ect...). Finally, *Franchising* is an excellent idea for investors who are looking to minimize risk while maximizing profit potential by purchasing a proven business model and exercising their executive prowess, usually by hiring people much more skilled than they are to manage it. That being said, I would like to suggest that when it comes to your *Shaved Ice* business you should avoid *Franchising.*

Unless the *Franchise* you're considering charges a *Franchise Fee* of zero dollars there is absolutely no reason why you should hobble yourself before your race for *Financial Independence* has begun by committing to pay a yearly *Franchise Fee.* Why not? One reason is that we are discussing a seasonal business. Unless you reside in a city like Phoenix, where it's constantly hot, you will most likely face being closed during the winter months. But if I'm to be perfectly candid the answer comes back to the nationally recognized brand I've built my business around, Tropical Sno. The best part about Tropical Sno? Peerless quality, protected territories and no *Franchise Fees.*

I could justify paying a *Franchise Fee* for a myriad of business models, but not a *Shaved Ice* business. Aside from learning how to properly build and pour the product there is almost nothing proprietary about the business model involved in selling *Shaved Ice*, nor should there be. While they obviously share some things in common different locations will have different needs, usually dictated by the customers or the environment in which the business is located. Smart entrepreneurs meet needs and solve problems on an individual basis, not with a cookie-cutter approach. With that in mind the biggest, most important reason I advise against paying a *Franchise Fee* is because you don't have to.

Hyde Park: A gold mine to call my own

By the time Ron called to suggest that I focus on a different location for my second season I was feeling a little dejected and openly considering abandoning my idea altogether. When he added that the different location he had in mind was freshly established, profitable, and actually for sale at that moment I balked. He doubled down and insisted that I go talk to the owner (whom I will refer to as John) as soon as possible. Apparently John was ready to sell his location after only a couple of months in business. Only half-jokingly I told him I was feeling the same way, but he pressed me further. He very much believed in the location John was selling and, though he didn't make a presentation of it at the time, he very much believed in me. I was hesitant, and un-convinced, but I agreed to go and talk to John.

It was the end of July and all over the Treasure Valley the *Shaved Ice* business was slowing down. It seems to defy logic but August is the wind down period for *Shaved Ice* businesses locally. This is mainly because families are busy preparing to send their kids back to school. As July was turning into August that year I drove down to John's shack which was situated at the end of a popular, heavily foot-trafficked business district in the affluent north end of Boise called Hyde Park. There was a line of customers so I took a seat at one of the many tables and simply observed the surroundings.

It wasn't hard to see why John was having so much success. Hyde Park is situated in the middle of neighborhood, within walking distance of a large city park and four schools. It's an inviting little business district that only spans two blocks, but packed into those two blocks at the time were three restaurants, two bars, a few eclectic antique shops, a book store, an ice cream parlor, and a very popular gas station. It seemed to me that each business had managed to achieve a look of both upscale exclusivity *and* down-home, welcoming attitude reminiscent of your favorite episode of *Cheers*. Everywhere I looked I saw smiling people spending their hard earned money. I fell in love with the place almost instantly.

After about twenty minutes John finished serving the last customer in line. I approached him and introduced myself. He invited me inside and began to tell me about Hyde Park and why he chose to put his building there. He had built the shack himself from donated construction lumber and he was very proud of it. He established a good working relationship with the land owners by paying his rent for the year in full and in advance. It was a risk to offer the rent up front like that but I understood why he took it. For a location like this I would've gladly done the same.

Anticipating my only real question he told me that his motivation to sell was not due to a lack of business. He was very much in love with his fiancé, a law student of some kind. She had been given an internship at a law firm in California and had to move there in September. He would be moving with her, it was as simple as that. I sat quietly for most of the time just listening as he told me about a couple of his previous business ventures, their success or failure, and his desire to move to California and enter into married life. He mentioned that I had been highly recommended by Ron, which genuinely flattered me. When he discovered that I had been selling cars for the last three years he excitedly launched into a narrative about an independent dealership he had started with a partner and how it ended in disaster. We talked animatedly about selling cars for over an hour, as car guys tend to do. The entire time he was serving a steady stream of customers through the window.

When he asked me what I thought (the subtle transition between polite conversation and business conversation) I was honest and straight to the point. I told him that I would love nothing more than to buy his business but I was afraid I had wasted his time. I couldn't scrape up the $15,000 he wanted for it. I couldn't even offer him $6,000! The extent of my liquid net worth was a measly $5,000 cash. I felt like the lowest creature on earth as I told him this and I stood up to take my leave, embarrassed and disheartened. To my absolute disbelief and amazement he replied,

"I think we can work something out."

I didn't dare speak. I just sat down and listened to his proposal.

If it was agreeable with me he would go home that night and draw up a contract for the sale of the business. $5,000 would be the full purchase price which would be due immediately. In exchange for this I would agree to let him run the business until the end of the season that year. He would keep all the proceeds and hand over ownership to me after he closed down that season. This would allow him to collect as much money as possible from his gold mine of a location. I was absolutely taken back by his generosity. I agreed at once and extended my hand.

That winter was a lean one for me. I scrimped and saved every cent I could while slaving away at my job for the last few months I would hold it. I was careful not to mistakenly tip my hand at work by mentioning that I planned to quit that spring which enabled me to save as much as I could in the interim. This helped boost my confidence as I made the decision to focus on my

Definite Major Purpose as opposed to that of my employer and, as I have already described, when the time came I was ready for it.

Well... as ready as one can be anyway.

5

"First they ignore you, then they laugh at you, then they fight you, then you win…"

– Mahatma Ghandi

Trials, Tribulations, and Suggestions

You've probably figured out by now that my path to *Financial Independence* was not without obstacles. Apart from the bad decisions I made along the way there were influences conspiring against my success that need to be addressed. Some of these influences were beyond my control. Some of these influences were completely within my control. These influences I speak of are not unique to me or my situation. I suspect that many current and would-be business people have experienced similar circumstances.

For example, whenever I work a shift at one of my locations some variation of the following exchange usually occurs:

Customer: *"Are you the owner?"*

Me: (proud and smiling) *"Yes I am."*

Customer: *"Well... Let me tell you about how so-and-so is the best/worst at their job!"*

As an enterprising business owner you should be eager to hear your customer's suggestions and criticisms. You should want to meet and exceed their expectations. But you can't exceed your customer's expectations without first knowing what they are. Get to know your customers and what they want. Encourage your employees to do the same. Address concerns immediately, especially if the customer you're speaking to is a *Regular*. Reassure your customers that any issue they have with your employees will be addressed immediately and then do exactly that. Become a humble servant to your customers. They will pay you for it.

Finally, I was not a success story right out of the gate. Learning from my mistakes has been instrumental on my journey to *Financial Independence*. That being said, I would like to share with you some of the most common mistakes I see people repeatedly make.

The Build and the Pour; the Hand vs. the Spoon

<u>Shaved Ice Specific Tip #4</u> – *Learn to properly build and pour Shaved Ice.*

How Not to Pour...

The most frequent complaint/compliment I hear from customers (especially new customers) is that the last time they had *Shaved Ice* the *Sno-rista* in charge of handling their order messed it all up by not properly pouring their syrup or not shaving the ice to the consistency they like. This is usually right after telling me that the *Shaved Ice* I just made for them was the best they've ever had in their life. I'm not joking or bragging. I've heard this a hundred times. But why? What have I done different to elicit such a response (and to hear it so often)? The answer: I've mastered the Build and the Pour.

Think of the Build and Pour as steps one and two of the complete path to a perfect *Shaved Ice*. The majority of people prefer to use their gloved hands to build and form the ice as it falls from the blade, lightly packing the snow into place so that the finished product resembles a quasi-firm, fluffy cotton candy, and melts in the mouth accordingly. This is what I like to refer to as the *Traditional Method* for making *Shaved Ice* as it is the most widely practiced in Hawaii, where modern *Shaved Ice* is from. If perfected, this method of building *Shaved Ice* will prove as valuable to the prospective business owner as learning the *Art of Selling* itself. The finished product is usually obnoxiously, shockingly huge in size. Often, the customer is unable to finish half of their would-be meal before it melts into a sweet soup in the bottom of their non-insulated cup. *Traditional Shaved Ice* is usually served in a thin, plastic cup-bowl hybrid called a *Flower Cup*, though I prefer using Tropical Sno's *Spill Stoppers* which allow for one major benefit that *Flower Cups* just can't buy: *Brand Recognition.*

Learning the *Traditional Method* of building *Shaved Ice* is important if you want to be legitimate in this business. Mastering it has earned me many dollars over the years because *Traditional Shaved Ice* enables the business owner to command a higher price than they otherwise might from using the same amount of product (sometimes less). However, not everyone is a fan of huge mountains of *Shaved Ice.* Most of my customers prefer something akin to what is presented on the menu, a cup of snow with a modest snow ball on top.

I was taught to build *Shaved Ice* with a spoon which I understand is uncommon. To this day that is the method I prefer. Using a spoon to build *Shaved Ice* enables me to complete an order more quickly than the *Traditional Method* and is necessary due to the high volume of business that my locations keep up with. Both methods are suitable and I encourage you to use whichever one feels more natural to you and makes the most sense for your particular location, always paying attention to what your customer demands.

The Traditional Method of building Shaved Ice.

vs.

The Spoon Method

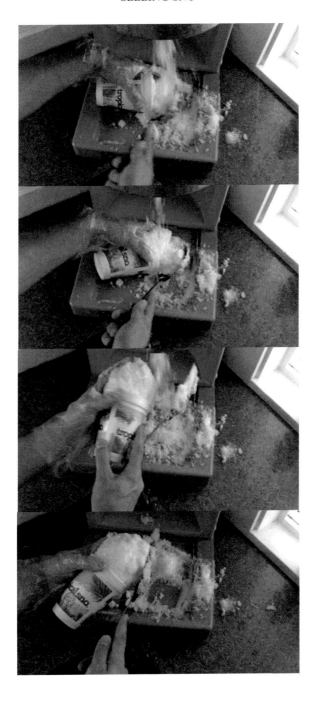

What spoon do I recommend over all others? The Ekco brand nylon slotted spoon. If you can find it.

How to Pour

The Pour is often mistaken for the easiest step. I've seen many people claim to know how to pour *Shaved Ice* only to blindly dump a bottle of syrup upside down on their effort and make the most ridiculous mess you've ever seen. The worst part being that only the top half of the thing is edible because the would-be *Snorista* holding the bottle didn't bother to make sure that even one drop of syrup hit the bottom of the cup!

The proper way to pour *Shaved Ice* is actually simple. When pouring *Shaved Ice* you must use your finger and the pour spout for control. Pour a controlled stream straight down the middle of your *Shaved Ice* until you hear or feel the syrup hit the bottom of the cup. After that you lightly cover the top with syrup and you're done. If the customer asks for heavy syrup wait a few seconds to let the syrup sink down and expand after the initial pour, hit the top with it again (lightly) and viola, you're done. It's as simple as that. Never grab the bottle by the side and blindly dump it upside down over the snow hoping that you'll create anything besides an unsatisfying mess. You won't. When pouring more than one flavor ***only use one*** to reach the bottom of the cup. Mind the structural integrity of your creation by not murdering it with multiple streams to the bottom. This is often the main cause of undesirable soupiness in the bottom of the cup, when your customer should be finishing off a cotton candy-like creation that melts in their mouth.

Finger on the spout...

Pour straight down until you hit the bottom of the cup...

Lightly cover the top and you're done!

<u>Shaved Ice Specific Tip #5</u> – *Let your ice blocks reach room temperature. Always have a block in the sink if you have one in the machine.*

Never take a frozen block of ice directly from the freezer and try to spin it on the machine. If you're successful you won't be for long. Spinning a solidly frozen block is the quickest way to damage your expensive machine, and possibly your face, as the teeth on the spike plate will only sink firmly and safely into a slightly tempered block. Freezer-temperature blocks will also freeze the blade, seriously hamper your productive abilities, and cause your line of would-be customers to disappear. A hint for freeing up clogged, frozen blades: warm water. Pour warm water over the blade until the offending ice chunk falls into the drip tray. Then read the following paragraph closely, twice.

Shaved Ice machines are meant to spin a slightly tempered block of ice. By slightly tempered I don't mean melting into a puddle. A soupy block ruins the texture of the ice and therefore the product you're about to present to your customer. Once a block is in the machine I usually leave it there, where it will continue to melt, though at a manageable rate. I rotate ice blocks between the freezer, sink, and machine in the event that one has melted too much. When I need to replace a block I do so with one from the sink. The second thing I do is pull a fresh frozen block from the freezer and allow it to temper. My advice is that you make this behavior a habit. If you always pull a block of ice out of the freezer when you replace your machine block you will rarely be caught with a frozen block which causes a frozen blade, or worse, a block frozen to the machine itself. (Hint: Use an ice chipper to unseat a block which has frozen to the machine.)

An ice block made from unfiltered water.

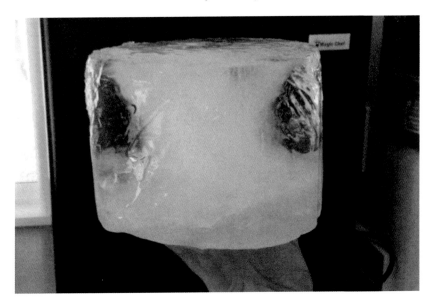

An ice block made from filtererd water.

Shaved Ice Specific Tip #6 – *Become a Sno-rista and put out a tip jar.*

If you're not setting out a tip jar for your patrons to show you how much they appreciate your skills you are short-changing yourself. I've found that a good *Sno-rista* will earn around 10% of the daily sales in tips if they have served their customers properly. If the good *Sno-rista* in question is also the owner of the enterprise that translates into an additional 10% on top of the day's sales. It really is a no-brainer. So what makes one a good *Sno-rista?* Here are a few thoughts on exactly that.

Think of your favorite bartender or barista. Why do you prefer their service over others? My favorite bartenders tend to be friendly, but not overly so. They usually don't have a cheesy fake smile for me. Their voice isn't louder or friendlier than it should be. They give me enough time to make my own decision while at the same time offering suggestions where, when, and if appropriate. They're knowledgeable about what flavors go well together. Often they recognize me and know what I want before I even order. From start to finish the transaction is pleasant and satisfying. When I leave them a tip there is no doubt that they have earned it.

Become a *Sno-rista*. Learn to gauge your customers and their moods and preferences. Don't be fake, be a chameleon. Mimic their mood and attitude. Be a friend to them for the short time they are with you. Listen to them with attention. Make the transaction as pleasant as possible for them. You will be amazed at just how much they will reward you for it.

Shaved Ice Specific Tip #7 – *Offer sugar-free flavors.*

Offering sugar free flavors is an easy way to attract regulars who otherwise wouldn't consider buying *Shaved Ice* at all. Some folks have diabetes. Some are more health conscious than others and go to great lengths not to consume any more sugar than necessary. As the owner of the business however, their motive should not concern you. Just their request for sugar-free syrup should be enough to compel you to make it. Also, make your sugar-free options from a selection of your most popular flavors. I always have at least three sugar-free choices to present to my customers when they request it. If they're not interested in what I've prepared I always ask for suggestions. Use *Splenda* or a generic equivalent to make your syrups. *Splenda* is the most requested brand of sweetener for the sugar-free crowd by far and it can be mixed cup for cup like sugar.

Shaved Ice Specific Tip #8 – *Build your Shaved Ice first and then pour it.*

I've found that when handling larger orders it's much easier to build my customer's *Shaved Ice* first and then pour it for them. This is beneficial for two reasons. First, it's more efficient. It keeps the line moving and enables me to serve more customers at once. The second reason is a little more subtle. People will often change their mind once or twice as they're standing in line. The time taken to build the whole order allows them to come to a decision without rushing them. Remember that business breeds business and people want to be seen. A crowd in front of your window is a good thing. While I am recommending a streamlining process for your serving routine, I'm not suggesting that you want to do whatever possible to rush through your line and chase everybody off.

While we're on the subject of customer etiquette I'd like to offer the following advice: Asking a hesitant customer, *"Do you know what size you're thinking?"* goes much further than simply saying *"What can I get for you?"*, *"What would you like?"*, or something along those lines. It is a much more polite way to get the customer thinking about what they actually want.

Pitfalls

Shaved Ice Specific Tip #9 – *Be a professional at all times.*

The most important thing to remember when dealing with every element surrounding your business is this: *Be a Professional.* This especially goes for your dealings with all people (land owners, customers, and employees). What you say can hurt you, just ask Donald Sterling. Whether you like it or not people love to sue you and steal your belongings in America. Instead of griping about how "unfair" that might be my suggestion is that you maintain constant vigilance against any possible attack with consistent professionalism. This means don't swear at or around customers/employees. In fact, don't lose your temper around them at all. Refrain from any comments that could be even slightly construed as *sexual*. Avoid arguments or discussions involving politics or religion at work, even with someone you think you agree with. Don't express opinions about controversial subjects in a way that you know will offend someone. In general, watch what you say and always be polite.

Shaved Ice Specific Tip #10 – *Be smarter than any potential threat/nemesis/competition.*

When dealing with your business you must make sure that every base is covered. Don't leave yourself, or your location, vulnerable and open to attack by some would-be rock star who thinks they can run your enterprise better than you. Threats can come in many forms but the two I'd like to focus on are competition from other *Prospective Owners* and *Regulation/Code Enforcers.*

The job of the *Regulation/Code Enforcer* is quite literally to shut down offending businesses. We have already discussed how to avoid them but it bears repeating. Don't give them a reason to shut you down when they come around. Be prepared by having your permits on display or at least ready to present to anyone who might come asking to see them.

The *Prospective Owner* is a different kind of threat. This is because they are motivated by the idea of taking over what's yours, namely your business and/or location. Often, they sell a different product or offer a non-edible service such as Emmissions Testing. Their one universally identifying feature is their desire to get in touch with your landlord any way possible. Their one universally identifying tactic is to contact your landlord and offer them a juicier lease payment than you currently pay. They typically target your employees with a prefabricated story hoping that your employee will cough up the landlord's contact information without you finding out about it. There are two ways to pre-empt these snakes. The first is to never share your landlord's contact information with anyone, especially your employees. The second is to make it clear to anyone you employ that contact information in general is never to be given out. Furthermore I tell my employees to be on the lookout for people who come around persistently pestering them for information so they can be identified by all employees and made example of.

Shaved Ice Specific Tip #11 – *Be very, VERY careful about whom you employ.*

It doesn't matter what product or service you offer, if you want your business to run without you someday you will have to trust it to your employees. I know trusting your business to a stranger is akin to trusting your baby to a stranger. The anxiety and potential disaster involved are enough to give any proud parent Acid-Reflux Disease. Therefore, take caution when considering anyone for employment. And it should go without saying that you should always check every reference provided by any potential candidate for employment.

I've had amazing employees and not-so-amazing employees. I've had employees who worked for me for three years and employees who worked for me for three minutes. In both cases their choices and behavior dictated the outcome. Keeping harmony between employees is an important factor in any establishment and can be a daunting challenge to the business owner that is not prepared to terminate someone's job on the spot. My suggestion when dealing with any drama involving employees is this: *Consider the business first.* Ask yourself if what you're considering will help or harm your business. If you find that the situation is harmful to your business take action and end someone's job immediately. Don't let it spiral out of your control to the detriment of your enterprise.

Always be crystal clear in what you expect from an employee in return for their labor. You, the business owner, are not responsible for offering up multiple second chances if they aren't living up to expectations. There are so many capable people looking for work that you will never have to bother with incompetence, provided you make the effort to locate those capable people.

When Good Help Goes Bad

Shaved Ice Specific Tip #12 – *Unless you are 100% sure (and I mean 100%, and sometimes even then) avoid partnerships at all costs.*

Many people have no clue that Steve Jobs was actually forced out of Apple, (a company he created with a partner) at one point. While he was able to rebound, re-take control of his company, and transform it from a huge money loser to a huge money maker, I would like to suggest that you never want to put yourself in a similar position.

I once had an amazing employee who could fix almost anything. We became friends after a few months and kept in touch when the *Shaved Ice* season ended. When he suggested that we form a partnership and establish a new location, one that he had already scouted out, I was hesitant. I agreed to do it, against my better judgment, because I could tell that it meant a lot to him to be taking his first entrepreneurial steps. But the experience was ultimately a disaster. The location was a huge failure and our friendship ended before the season did.

Even the appearance or illusion of a partnership can be devastating. Well meaning friends can become enemies overnight when it comes to a business venture because (among many other things) everyone has a different idea of what it means to be successful. For some it could mean rolling around in gold coins as if they were Scrooge McDuck, having expended little to no effort. If this fairytale scenario doesn't present itself quickly don't be surprised when things get ugly. For others, their labor is viewed as the currency by which they have right to the business. Still others might have leverage over you by way of having control of something the business requires to function. I'd like to suggest that you nip any potential event in the bud by avoiding partnerships altogether. Simply put, two (or worse, more) people running a business means two or more very different plans for that business.

Shaved Ice Specific Tip #13 – *When it comes to your business, Comprehensive Insurance coverage is a **must**.*

Liability Insurance protects your landlord from any potential lawsuits involving the injury of your customers. Most landlords require that you purchase some level of *Liability Insurance* as a condition of whatever lease you are able to negotiate. *Comprehensive Insurance* covers the total destruction or theft of your belongings due to whatever unforeseen circumstance you weren't prepared for. For this reason alone it is very important to have *Comprehensive Insurance* protecting your building, machines, and inventory. This type of insurance is usually very reasonably priced and simple to understand. A worthy insurance agent once explained it to me like this: If your business burned down today and was a total loss how much money would you need to rebuild it exactly as it was? You need to make sure that you insure your business for **at least** that amount.

How Do I Expand?

If you are fortunate enough to experience the rush of emotions that comes with the establishment of a successful, profitable business you might find yourself asking the following question: How do I expand? The short answer is that you expand by duplicating the characteristics of your flagship location *in other equally suitable locations.* Ask yourself, what makes your main location successful?

I knew that I could expect a profitable season for my second year at Hyde Park. Because of this I made it a point during the winter to scout out a new location for my first building. I focused on moving my original building to a solid location with similar characteristics. I found one that was close and when summer arrived I moved the unit onto it, commencing my first season as a business owner with two separate locations. While it was much better than the previous spot, the new location suffered from a lack of visibility and as a result didn't perform nearly as well as it should have, and definitely nowhere near as well as Hyde Park.

During the first month of business the following summer Hyde Park nearly achieved its purchase price in terms of sales. As you might imagine, I was ecstatic. The only problem was my other struggling location. I found myself shelling out money earned at one location to prop up the other, a serious red flag.

Shaved Ice Specific Tip #14 – *Robbing Peter to pay Paul is called stealing.*

Don't steal from yourself. Don't loot one successful location to subsidize the folly of another. At the end of the day you're simply losing money. Cut your losses and consider the experience a lesson learned. Though there are obviously exceptions, my experience is that if a location you planned on turning into a profit producing monster hasn't manifest that characteristic after two months (provided you open for business May 1st) it's probably time to start scouting out a different location for next season. You might even find one as soon as you start looking which can inspire the urge to pick up and move your enterprise mid-season. A word of caution needs to be offered here. Though I will not use the word *never*, I will say that it is not advisable to uproot a building and switch locations mid-season. Only do this if one, your lease permits it, two, you can afford it, and three, you have no other choice.

Shaved Ice Specific Tip #15 – *Take the time to work random shifts at your locations.*

I worked Hyde Park as much as I could during the first two seasons mostly because I wanted to familiarize myself with my new customers and listen to their suggestions (which aren't always winners). I would like to suggest you do the same. My experience is that paying customers, especially *Regulars*, enjoy having a conversation with the owner of a business they frequent. It gives them a sense of community. Often, they can provide insight about how your employees behave while you're away. Also, some parents are naturally uneasy about anyone who comes in contact with their kids, especially if they're trying to sell them something. A smiling face and pleasing personality go a long way toward minimizing those legitimate worries.

Shaved Ice Specific Tip #16 – *Maintain regular business hours.*

Nothing pisses off a potential *Regular* quite like showing up at their establishment of choice and seeing that it's not open for business when it should be. If you have employees schedule shifts so that bathroom breaks and other nuisances do not become a costly problem. If you have to leave the shack, for even a minute, place a sign in the window telling your customers that you'll be right back. Only don't expect them to wait. Few actually do. They are much more likely to take their business to an establishment that respects the fact that they want to spend money on *their terms*, on *their time*.

Expanding on Expanding

Shaved Ice Specific Tip #17 – *Become a digital marketer for your business.*

Groupon, Facebook, Instagram, Google, Yelp, Linkedin, Go Daddy... Get the picture? Keeping up with digital marketing, including social networking, may seem like a chore but it's a chore worth keeping current on. The greatest chance of spreading the word about your business to as many people as possible (who you would otherwise never come in contact with) is through the internet. Whether you know it or not many people actually use these services frequently to determine what their next boredom killer should be. Help them to decide to meet up at your little hotspot of a business by offering incentives through social networks. Include photos of your latest creations for them to drool over. Make your business easy to find with the help of Google Maps. Bottom line: in 2015 your business needs an online presence. If you don't have one (even if it's only a simply Facebook page) make establishing one a priority.

Sometimes expanding is not as simple as scouting a potential location, approaching the land owner, making a friend, and striking a deal. Sometimes the best locations are situated on "publicly owned" lands such as parks which are usually administered by either the City or State. This means that (if they allow vendors on their land) you will have to deal with a bureaucracy and its assorted rules and regulations. Each City/State will have its own norms and traditions but this is usually not a problem if you only plan on selling *Shaved Ice* for a simple reason that we have briefly touched on.

Shaved Ice Specific Tip #18 – *In many states Shaved Ice is not regulated/designated "low risk" by the health dept.*

If you're going to be successful you will need to use every tool available to you. One tool that has been especially helpful to me is Tip #18. Check with the health department where you live and determine what regulations apply to *Shaved Ice* as soon as you put this book down if you haven't already.

6

"And here is the prime condition of success, the great secret. Concentrate your energy, thoughts and capital exclusively upon the business in which you are engaged in. Having begun in one line, resolve to fight it out on that line; to lead in it. Adopt every improvement, have the best machinery and know the most about it."

– Andrew Carnegie

Building an Empire

Building an empire of *Shaved Ice* shacks requires planning and preparation. I plotted out the locations of every shack in and around my hometown, regardless of what brand of syrup they sold, to determine exactly how they measured up to each other. I bought large street maps of Boise and the surrounding areas which I hung on the wall of my "command center", an entire room of my house dedicated to Tropical Sno and the idea of building my business. With the help of Ron's wisdom and guidance I soon knew the exact location of every snow shack worth mentioning in the Boise area. I used colored thumb tacks to map out the location of each one within in a 30 mile radius, reserving the white ones to designate mine versus the competition which I separated into two categories: those I was interested in owning and those I was not interested in owning. The locations drawing my interest were divided further into those I would have to acquire versus those I would have to establish, providing they met the conditions of the aforementioned *Anatomy of a Good Location.*

The guidance of my mentors Ron and Darlene was crucial during this period. They had wisely invested in large walk-in freezers a few years before I met them in order to sell ice to the growing number of Tropical Sno dealers around Boise. Thank goodness too, because I could not make enough ice to keep up with the demand of my growing number of shacks. Ron provided the necessary introductions/recommendations for a few of my acquisitions while Darlene went out of her way to provide ice and advice, both of which I used as much as I could. With their help I was soon managing six locations.

Sweet Success

Shaved Ice Specific Tip #19 – *Look to the city's parks for opportunity. Establish a working relationship with a Government Entity.*

One of my most beneficial acquisitions involved a *Shaved Ice* business in the city park. I would like to suggest that a busy park environment (usually owned by the City or State) should be one of the first locations you consider. Parks with swimming pools or water facilities are great for *Shaved Ice* businesses because they attract tons of hot, thirsty people. There is usually plenty of provided shade and seating. Organizations like children's sports teams and the YMCA routinely gather in parks to facilitate large groups. The citizenry often demands quality vendors in their city parks and as a result many Parks and Recreation departments frequently put out RFPs (Request For Proposal) seeking enterprising business owners who can pass muster. Seize this opportunity.

If you're going to put together a submission, application, or proposal for a *Government Entity* like the City or State you'll want to bring your A-Game. This is where **Tip #9** really comes in handy. Often they want to see some kind of proof of liquidity (a photocopy of your bank account for example). Sometimes they will even request to pull your credit. You must either be prepared for these things or be prepared to find a way around them (which can be done, believe it or not). Make timely rent payments a priority. Better yet, pay your entire lease for the year up front and in full. This is usually pretty easy because:

Shaved Ice Specific Tip #20 – *Government Entities usually dramatically undervalue the rent.*

When a property owner offers favorable lease terms up front, without you having to negotiate, politely accept them and say thank you. Occasionally this happens with private land owners, though it is much more likely to happen with *Government Entities*, which are notoriously out of the loop when it comes to the actual market on real estate. You could spend time complaining about this fact or you could use it to your advantage. Guess which path I recommend...

Just My Luck

"Luck is what happens when preparation meets opportunity"

— Seneca, Roman philosopher, mid-1st century AD

Establishing a working relationship with a City Parks and Recreation department as a vendor has been a lucrative decision for me. Quality vendors are not as easy to come by as you might first imagine. One year the City called to inform me that they couldn't get in touch with a certain vendor who normally set up in a different park. They were sick of attempting to contact them and wanted to know if I would be interested in taking over the location in addition to what I had already committed to that summer. I agreed at once, even though I didn't have a building I could commit to the cause, the whole time marveling at my luck. In reality luck had little to do with it. They were simply looking to someone they knew would get the job done. Being the right person, in the right place, doing the right things at the right time enabled me to take advantage of this opportunity.

I didn't let them down either. I wasn't worried about where I would find a building on such short notice because for the previous two years I had established a working relationship with a local shed mover. I remembered him mentioning that he occasionally came across sheds which were abandoned or otherwise ownerless and for sale, usually at a deep discount. I called him to ask if any such shed was available and was delighted when he informed me that there was. The best part about this particular shed was that it was already wired for electricity and available for immediate delivery at a bargain basement price. The only drawback was that some kids had broken into it and lit off a series of fireworks, causing an unsightly burn on the floorboard. The inside would need a little TLC. Aside from that the building was nearly new. I made an appointment to check it out and after a cursory glance (where I estimated the damage to be very minimal and easy to clean/cover up) I bought it on the spot and had him deliver it to the park where I cleaned it up in a weekend and converted it into a building fit for business.

That year I poured a new concrete patio down in Hyde Park, where my little building made of donated construction lumber was beginning to fall apart. The floor had been all but pounded clear through to the ground by three seasons of serious business. The patio, cobbled together from pieces of granite and marble countertop and brick glue, had been stomped to bits by all of the heavy traffic. What used to be a cute idea had now become treacherous sand pit with sharp granite pieces poking up from it. It needed to be replaced. Due to my rapidly depleting cash hoard the dilapidated building, with its badly suffering floor, would have to survive for another year.

I needed to solve my patio problem cheaply, so I began scouring Craigslist to look for a reputable concrete company that was willing to barter in part for their services. To my surprise there was more than one. After meeting a couple of different contractors I selected an outfit to work with. This particular company had placed an ad expressing interest in bartering their services for vehicles. At the time I had two vehicles: a Cadillac which was worth something and an old Ford pickup which was worth nothing. While I was loathe to do it, I drove down to Hyde Park in my Cadillac to meet with the contractor. After measuring the area and discussing exactly what type of concrete I was interested in purchasing we settled on a price for the pad. Having accomplished that, I mentioned his ad and asked him to consider my car and what he might allow me for it in the deal, kind of like how a prospective customer sneaks in their trade after determining the bottom dollar of their desired car at a dealership. At first he didn't seem interested and I was thinking I had made a mistake. But then he mentioned that his wife favored larger cars like mine. He couldn't promise anything, but he would bring it up to her and see what she thought about it. At the dealership this was an objection I was used to hearing. It's usually coughed up by someone as a last ditch effort to escape with their wallet intact before doing something they might later regret. I told him that I understood.

I was a little surprised when he sent me a text message the next day asking me to bring the car back to Hyde Park for his wife to see and test drive. As they were looking over my well cared for car, the glances exchanged between them told me all I needed to know. She liked it at once. Salesman that I am, I tailored my walk around specifically to her. After a short test drive they returned and told me that they would give me $2,000 toward the concrete for my car, which was about what I expected. I agreed at once, signed the title away, and kissed my baby goodbye. She had served me well for over four years at that point and I felt I had received more than my money's worth. The next day, as I watched my new concrete pad being poured, I couldn't help but smile. The whole time I was thinking, "This is how entrepreneurs solve problems!"

The beginning of the end for the patio in Hyde Park...

Stacking Assets

Around this time I discovered that word of my success had been spreading. I began to be contacted by different shack owners who wanted advice, and among other things, suggestions as to how they could achieve the same amount of success that I had. One of these owners, a true gentleman, would provide another opportunity for expansion.

When the housing bubble of 2007/08 popped quite a few people (including myself) were left holding the bag in the form of mortgages in which the underlying asset had fallen by 50% or more. Jim was one such homeowner. Both Jim and his wife had amazing credit to go along with their amazing jobs. As the housing market started boiling around 2005 they didn't think twice about using their credit to "purchase" a couple extra income properties, and for a few years the extra income was a welcome addition to the family. But then the market began to tank. They were able to sell one house quick enough, though at a loss to its original purchase price which included the sacrificed cash down payment. Jim made up for the lost income by putting in extra hours at his job, which worked for about a year. Then Jim's job disappeared, a victim of the larger contracting economy. To compound matters, Jim's renter found *himself* without a job a short time later and announced that he would have to move out. Jim realized he would have to put his rental house on the market, where it would sit for two long years, shedding the weight of his hard earned equity with each passing day as the mortgage payments made a quick and easy meal of his savings.

Jim was open to all suggestions when it came to supplemental income by that point. Having three high school age kids, all actively looking for a summer job, only lent weight to the idea of opening a *Shaved Ice* business when he was first presented with it. Much like my own experience, his first location was not a success. We met for the first time that year. Jim appeared at my window down in Hyde Park and after describing his location asked for some simple advice, which I was happy to offer. When the next season arrived he moved his shack to a *Good Location* across from a high school, where it would establish itself as a legitimate business while at the same time providing his children with the employment/income they were already seeking.

Shortly after Jim's rental property sold (at the bottom of the market) he was presented with a long sought after out of state job offer. Intent on moving with his wife to wherever his new job offer might take him, Jim made the decision to sell his freshly established, and well-performing, *Shaved Ice* shack. As one of the first people to be contacted about the fact his business was on the market I was able to capitalize on the opportunity quickly and secure the location before the season began that year.

Tiger's Blood Flavored Sorbet…?

That fall, after the season was finished, Ron offered me the first hint of the fact that he would soon be retiring. He called me to his house telling me that he had a surprise for me. He knew that I had been on the lookout for a new building for Hyde Park. After another season the original building was nearly unusable. I was spending a majority of my free time scouring the market for a reasonable deal on a new building, preferably one wired for 220 volts so that I could buy Ron's soft serve machine and offer Tropical Sno's amazing sorbet product, *Soft Ice*. I saw the potential to grow the business by becoming the only *Shaved Ice* shack in Boise to offer *Soft Ice*, and it has since become one of the best decisions that I've made in regards to that location. The best decision has the distinction of being made by my mentor, who called me that afternoon to invite me to go look at a building he had been scouting.

A surprise awaited me instead. When I pulled into Ron's driveway the building was already sitting there, all 200 square feet of it. It was more than three times larger than any *Shaved Ice* shack I had ever seen, with drive-up serving windows on both sides. I parked my car and just stared. I almost didn't notice Ron standing there smiling, observing me.

"What do you think?" he asked as I was approaching the building..

"I thought we were going to *look* at a building...!" was all I could say.

"I think your search is over." He said triumphantly.

"I can't afford this." I said as I opened up the door to have a look inside. It had clearly been used as a drive through coffee stand. Some machinery had been left behind as well as plenty of coffee grounds. The floor was bare with the subflooring exposed. In the middle of the floor was a large hole which had been purposely cut out to expose the ground below, a crude version of a drop-safe. The piece of subflooring which fit inside it was lying in the corner, disturbed by the recent move. I could see two 220 volt power outlets on opposite sides of the interior. This building would have no problem accommodating a soft serve machine.

"Sure you can. I only paid five thousand dollars for it. Dump some money off to me over the winter when you can and it's yours. In the meantime you can fix it up here, right where it sits." He said.

I turned my attention from the building to Ron. He was gauging me in his patient way. This man who had mentored me through the last four years as I built my self-sustaining business empire had already given me so much, but for him to offer this was simply over the top. Yet I knew to refuse or question his generosity would have been supremely disrespectful. I could have given him a hug. Humbled and nearly speechless, I walked over to where he was standing and gratefully shook his hand.

"Thank you," was all I could manage to say.

By spring of the following year I was ready to place my new, freshly fixed up building in Hyde Park. Because his vinyl fencing business was beginning to demand more of his time, my brother (who briefly dabbled in the business at my suggestion) decided to sell his location and asked if I would help him do it. I agreed immediately. By asking for my help he sparked anew the idea of selling in my own mind. As summer approached that year I found myself increasingly wondering, "What I could sell one of my locations for…?"

7

"The final step in becoming an entrepreneur involves selling your business."

– Robert Kiyosaki

Selling the Dream

(Photo courtesy of Clint Nye)

Shaved Ice Specific Tip #21 – *Events like concerts, festivals, and fairs can provide more income in one day than you ever thought possible.*

Ron bought an enclosed concessions trailer and a couple kiosks in order to vend at one of Idaho's largest outdoor stadiums, the Idaho Center, a few years before I came along. For the previous eight years you could find him there rocking out every blazing hot midsummer outdoor music festival/freak show the venue was able to procure with the help of his family and several employees. Individual concerts were also a huge source of income, though some were much more lucrative than others. The biggest event was the family friendly (i.e. no alcohol allowed) and aptly named God and Country Rally, a one day event where Ron would routinely sell between five and six thousand dollars of *Shaved Ice* in a single day. Yes, you read that sentence correctly: Between *five and six thousand dollars* in sales for one day's work, selling *Shaved Ice* on a hot day.

But after more than 20 years of building and selling shacks, mentoring newbies like me and working huge events, Ron was ready to retire. He mentioned this to me one day, about a month before my sixth season in business. He told me that he had made the decision to sell his trailer, kiosks, machines, and basically everything else that went along with his Idaho Center vending gig. He would make the necessary introductions to the current concessions coordinators and do everything in his power to sheppard the transition to a new owner, a transition which he expected no problems with. That being said, would I be interested in purchasing his equipment from him and taking on the challenge and responsibility?

Events are a massive undertaking because of the number of

people involved but they are usually well worth the time and effort spent. A major bonus to large events is that you can often raise your prices to ridiculous levels. Remember that corn dog you paid six bucks for at the fair? Imagine a never ending line of fifty sun-baked concert goers and you will have some idea of what to expect if you ever take your enterprise to the next level and become a vendor for large events. The best part about large events is that they can be found in every city in America and their organizers are all looking for vendors to show up, sell food, pay them (the event organizers) a usually exorbitant cut, then leave.

The fact that he wanted me to take over such a large responsibility inspired feelings of pride and accomplishment in and of itself. I agreed that I would do it. But committing to this deal meant that I would need to say goodbye to a few of my beloved locations. I would not be able to keep up with the responsibilities of running all of them *and* the demands of the Idaho Center. If I was to properly take on Ron's vending gig and pay it the attention and respect it deserved, I was going to have to free up some of my time, and that meant selling some of my assets.

Shaved Ice Specific Tip #22 – *Keep accurate records of all sales/expenses to show any potential buyers of your business. When you find a buyer, do everything you can to sheppard the transition.*

If you're planning on selling your business you should have a good idea of its finances. I use a simple notebook to keep track of sales and save every receipt to keep track of expenses, which I check against my business bank account. With a few exceptions I have kept every record of my business-related transactions going back to the year I started. Accurate accounting is a simple and essential tool in determining whether a business is profitable. When it comes time to sell, accurate accounting records are priceless.

Also, when selling your *Shaved Ice* business you want to do everything you can to make the transition as smooth as possible for the new owner. That means working hand in glove with them as well as your current landlord as landlords are naturally leery of a prospective new tenant. Do them and yourself a favor by politely qualifying your prospective customer. Do they have references? Do they have enough money to cover the lease if things don't go as planned? Do they have experience managing a business? Things your landlord might ask them. None of these are a deal breaker but you want to be sure that you're dealing with someone who is able to pay you in full and make a positive impression on your landlord to the degree that your landlord requires. After all, if the landlord and prospective new owner don't hit it off you can kiss your sale goodbye.

Saying Goodbye

I am a huge fan of the free and unregulated market which means that I am a huge fan of Craigslist. I highly recommend using it if you have anything to sell. Having decided that I would ultimately sell three of my locations, I set about making a Craigslist ad for the first one. The same day I put my business on the market many interested parties, including the person who would eventually buy it, responded to the ad. I made a point to speak to each of them, feeling them out through my qualifying questions, gauging their readiness to take on the responsibility of business ownership, and perhaps most importantly, determining which were seriously looking (and able) to buy versus which were shopping for information they might use to start their own enterprise from scratch as I had done so many years before.

Originally I intended to present one location at a time without informing my prospective customer that I owned multiple locations, a few of which were not for sale. But after meeting with the first serious prospective buyer I decided that I would offer everyone I deemed suitable a shot at buying any of the three locations that I intended to sell. This would keep things simple. I would only have to place a single ad to do it, culling my prospective customers from the list of those initially interested enough to reply to the ad (which I placed a few months before the season began). I priced them a few thousand dollars apart based on my record of the previous years' sales. I figured that a fair asking price amounted to what the location in question would *net* (in terms of profit) after the first year of ownership, thereby reasonably guaranteeing (while not explicitly promising) a 100% return on investment in the first year if run properly. My logic must have made an appealing sales pitch. I sold all three locations before the season began.

Conclusion

Starting a small business isn't for everyone. Selling it can be even harder. There are so many variables involved that it is easy to become confused and discouraged. I believe that I've had an advantage over most people due to my experience working in my family's restaurant and the guidance I've been provided by my amazing mentors Ron and Darlene. But don't let inexperience deter you. Don't let anything deter you for that matter.

Now, more than ever, people I meet for the first or second time at my window are asking me detailed questions about why I chose to get into the business of selling *Shaved Ice*. While some are simply making idle conversation, others are posing long-held, serious questions. They're seeking *Financial Independence* and they rightfully see owning a *Shaved Ice* business as a legitimate path to achieve that noble goal. They often have teenage children and see the opportunity for them to be employed while learning ethics standards and management skills. They want a legitimate, simple, effective, way to supplement their income. They don't want a multi-level scam where they have to share their earnings with whatever goon convinced them to pay for the privilege of being employed. They want to go into business for themselves. And they want to do so with an initial investment that doesn't reduce them to paupers.

When I'm approached by people who are openly looking for information about buying or establishing a *Shaved Ice* business I give them the same information that I've presented in this book, often suggesting other books which have helped me immensely along the way. Not everyone will follow the exact formula I'm prescribing and that's ok. Your business is exactly that, *your business*. Take what you can use and leave the rest. Use what works for you and your business.

I wish you well on your quest for *Financial Independence*. Be vigilant. Be bold. Be daring. *Financial Independence* is possible. More than that, it is *necessary*. Pay absolutely no attention to visionless haters attempting to convince you otherwise. Their opinions will have no effect on your life unless you let them. Owning and operating a small business has been one of the best decisions I have ever made. For me, *Financial Independence* is a reality. And would you like to know what the best part about the whole thing is?

I did it all by Selling Sno.

ABOUT THE AUTHOR

Aaron Mayovsky is a writer, musician, and entrepreneur as well as a student of economics, history, politics, music, and the Spanish language. He lives in Boise, Idaho where he owns and operates a multi-location *Shaved Ice* business. During the off-season he enjoys composing and recording original music with his dad.